Puppet Essentials

Get up and running quickly using the power of
Puppet to manage your IT infrastructure

Felix Frank

BIRMINGHAM - MUMBAI

Puppet Essentials

First published: November 2014

Production reference: 1171114

Published by Packt Publishing Ltd.
Livery Place
35 Livery Street
Birmingham B3 2PB, UK.

ISBN 978-1-78398-748-1

www.packtpub.com

Credits

Author
Felix Frank

Reviewers
Ger Apeldoorn

Thomas Dao

Brian Moore

Josh Partlow

Commissioning Editor
Edward Gordon

Acquisition Editor
Sam Wood

Content Development Editor
Sweny M. Sukumaran

Technical Editor
Mrunal M. Chavan

Copy Editors
Deepa Nambiar

Stuti Srivastava

Project Coordinator
Rashi Khivansara

Proofreaders
Simran Bhogal

Maria Gould

Ameesha Green

Paul Hindle

Indexers
Mariammal Chettiyar

Tejal Soni

Graphics
Ronak Dhruv

Production Coordinator
Manu Joseph

Cover Work
Manu Joseph

About the Author

Felix Frank has used and programmed computers for most of his life. During and after his Computer Science diploma, he gained on-the-job experience as a system administrator, server operator, and open source software developer. Of his 10-year career, he spent 5 years as a Puppet power user. For almost a year, he intensified his learning by contributing source code and actively participating in several conferences. This is his first foray into writing books and is a work of great effort and sacrifice.

Acknowledgments

I'd like to thank my editors, Sam Wood, Sweny M. Sukumaran, and Mrunal M. Chavan, for their ongoing support and for making this title possible in the first place. This book would not be what it is without the amazing feedback from my reviewers, Ger Apeldoorn, Brian Moore, Josh Partlow, and Thomas Dao.

I'd also like to thank a number of Puppet Labs employees for their kind feedback and ongoing support—Andrew Parker, Adrien Thebo, Dawn Foster, Joshua Partlow, Josh Cooper, Henrik Lindberg, Charlie Sharpsteen, Kylo Ginsberg, Ethan Brown, Rob Reynolds, Jeff McCune, and Eric Sorenson. Special thanks to Luke Kanies for creating Puppet and dedicating so many resources to this amazing community.

Further thanks to Waltraut Niepraschk and the entire data center staff at DESY Zeuthen for getting me on track with the central management of Unix servers. Also, thanks to MPeXnetworks for giving me the opportunity to learn more about Puppet and ultimately helping me write this very book.

About the Reviewers

Ger Apeldoorn is a freelance Puppet consultant and teaches official Puppet Labs courses in the Netherlands. He has helped implement Puppet in many companies, both open source and Enterprise, and has given a presentation on *Manageable Puppet Infrastructure* at PuppetConf and other conferences. He recently found out that writing about himself in third person can be a bit awkward.

Thomas Dao has spent over two decades playing around with various Unix flavors as a Unix administrator, build and release engineer, and configuration manager. He is passionate about open source software and tools, so Puppet was something he naturally gravitated toward. Currently employed in the telecommunications industry as a configuration analyst, he also divides some of his time as a technical editor at `devops.ninja`.

> I would like to thank my lovely wife, whose patience with me while I'm glued to my monitor gives me the inspiration to pursue my passions, and my dog, Bento, who is always by my side, giving me company.

Brian Moore is a senior product engineer, a father of two, and a quintessential hacker. He began coding at the age of 12. His early love for everything technological led to a job with Apple shortly after high school. Since that time, he has worked with a series of start-ups and tech companies, taking on interesting technical challenges. He was also the technical reviewer for *Rhomobile Beginner's Guide, Packt Publishing*. When not working on new development projects, he can often be found off-roading in a remote Southern California desert in his Baja Bug.

Josh Partlow is a software developer working in Portland, OR. He started working as a freelance consultant in the early 90s and has worked on a variety of database, web, and networking projects in Java, Perl, and Ruby, developing primarily on Linux platforms. He helped found OpenSourcery and currently works at Puppet Labs on the core Puppet project itself. He lives in Portland with his wife, Julia, and their two cats, Fred and Ethel, who are mostly nothing like their namesakes.

www.PacktPub.com

Support files, eBooks, discount offers, and more

For support files and downloads related to your book, please visit www.PacktPub.com.

Did you know that Packt offers eBook versions of every book published, with PDF and ePub files available? You can upgrade to the eBook version at www.PacktPub.com and as a print book customer, you are entitled to a discount on the eBook copy. Get in touch with us at service@packtpub.com for more details.

At www.PacktPub.com, you can also read a collection of free technical articles, sign up for a range of free newsletters and receive exclusive discounts and offers on Packt books and eBooks.

https://www2.packtpub.com/books/subscription/packtlib

Do you need instant solutions to your IT questions? PacktLib is Packt's online digital book library. Here, you can search, access, and read Packt's entire library of books.

Why subscribe?

- Fully searchable across every book published by Packt
- Copy and paste, print, and bookmark content
- On demand and accessible via a web browser

Free access for Packt account holders

If you have an account with Packt at www.PacktPub.com, you can use this to access PacktLib today and view 9 entirely free books. Simply use your login credentials for immediate access.

Dedicated to Patrizia for all the years of love and support.

Table of Contents

Preface

The software industry is changing and so are its related fields. Old paradigms are slowly giving way to new roles and shifting views on what the different professions should bring to the table. The DevOps trend pervades evermore workflows. Developers set up and maintain their own environments, and operations raise automation to new levels and translate whole infrastructures to code.

A steady stream of new technologies allows for more efficient organizational principles. One of these newcomers is Puppet. Its fresh take on server configuration management caused rapid adoption and distribution throughout the industry. In the few years of its existence, Puppet has managed to rally thousands of users who employ it in numerous contexts to achieve manifold results. While it is not the only configuration management system available, it is certainly the most widespread by now.

From its specialized language to the system that makes it work, Puppet has innovated and rapidly conquered the software industry. Its extendible structure, paired with a large and helpful community, has made Puppet a powerhouse of easy configuration. The more well known a software is, the greater the chance that Puppet will deploy and configure it out of the box.

Puppet's own learning curve is not sharp, and the available documentation is not only extensive, but also of high quality. Nevertheless, even experienced programmers and administrators can face difficulties at some point. Advanced use might require the navigation of some intricacies that stem from Puppet's unique modeling approach.

This book aims at teaching you all that is required to tap not only the basics of Puppet, but also the very ideas and principles of Puppet-based designs. Sophisticated tooling is presented in order to enable efficient and productive use. You are introduced to and familiarized with a range of Puppet-centric technologies.

What this book covers

Chapter 1, Writing Your First Manifests, gives you an introduction to the core concepts of Puppet, including a syntax tutorial. You will learn how to write and use Puppet manifests within a few pages.

Chapter 2, The Master and Its Agents, provides you with a quick how-to guide in order to set up all the components required for a distributed Puppet infrastructure. It will teach you how to create the master, an agent, and set up Passenger with Apache or Nginx.

Chapter 3, A Peek Under the Hood – Facts, Types, and Providers, gives you a summary of the core components that give Puppet its flexibility as well as its ease of use and extension. It will help you understand the principles of Puppet's function.

Chapter 4, Modularizing Manifests with Classes and Defined Types, teaches you the most important structural elements of Puppet manifests. You will learn how to use them for best results.

Chapter 5, Extending Your Puppet Infrastructure with Modules, gives you a tour of downloadable extensions along with providing you with a guide to create your own. You will learn how to extend Puppet for your specific needs.

Chapter 6, Leveraging the Full Toolset of the Language, teaches you how to interpret and use language features beyond the basics.

Chapter 7, Separating Data from Code Using Hiera, provides you with an introduction to the powerful configuration data storage that comes with Puppet. You will learn how to naturally model your infrastructure in a hierarchy.

Chapter 8, Configuring Your Cloud Application with Puppet, gives you a superposition of the skills you have acquired. It will help you gain some specialized insights into how to take centralized control of your cloud through Puppet.

What you need for this book

To follow the examples, it is sufficient to use a computer with enough resources to run two or more virtual machine instances. The virtualization guests should have a connection to the Internet and with each other. The configuration examples are tailored to the Debian GNU/Linux operating system in Version 7 with the code name "Wheezy".

Who this book is for

This book assumes that you have no prior Puppet knowledge. You should have a sound technical background. Experience with the GNU/Linux command line is required. Existing programming skills are recommended. This book is also suitable for beginners or intermediate Puppet users who wish to expand their knowledge about the software.

Conventions

In this book, you will find a number of text styles that distinguish between different kinds of information. Here are some examples of these styles and an explanation of their meaning.

Code words in text, database table names, folder names, filenames, file extensions, pathnames, dummy URLs, user input, and Twitter handles are shown as follows: "If you do this, Puppet will include the full path to the newly created .dot file in its output."

A block of code is set as follows:

```
digraph Resource_Cycles {
  label = "Resource Cycles"
"File[/etc/haproxy/haproxy.cfg]" -> "Service[haproxy]" -> "File[/etc/
haproxy]" -> "File[/etc/haproxy/haproxy.cfg]"
}
```

When we wish to draw your attention to a particular part of a code block, the relevant lines or items are set in bold:

```
package {
    $apache_package:
        ensure => 'installed'
}
```

Any command-line input or output is written as follows:

```
root@puppet# puppet cert clean agent
Info: Caching certificate for agent
Notice: Revoked certificate with serial 18
Notice: Removing file Puppet::SSL::Certificate agent at '/var/lib/
puppet/ssl/ca/signed/agent.pem'
Notice: Removing file Puppet::SSL::Certificate agent at '/var/lib/
puppet/ssl/certs/agent.pem'
```

New terms and **important words** are shown in bold. Words that you see on the screen, for example, in menus or dialog boxes, appear in the text like this: "It's safer to click on the **Project URL** link near the top of the module description."

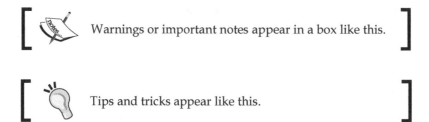

Warnings or important notes appear in a box like this.

Tips and tricks appear like this.

Reader feedback

Feedback from our readers is always welcome. Let us know what you think about this book—what you liked or disliked. Reader feedback is important for us as it helps us develop titles that you will really get the most out of.

To send us general feedback, simply e-mail feedback@packtpub.com, and mention the book's title in the subject of your message.

If there is a topic that you have expertise in and you are interested in either writing or contributing to a book, see our author guide at www.packtpub.com/authors.

Customer support

Now that you are the proud owner of a Packt book, we have a number of things to help you to get the most from your purchase.

Downloading the example code

You can download the example code files from your account at http://www.packtpub.com for all the Packt Publishing books you have purchased. If you purchased this book elsewhere, you can visit http://www.packtpub.com/support and register to have the files e-mailed directly to you.

Errata

Although we have taken every care to ensure the accuracy of our content, mistakes do happen. If you find a mistake in one of our books—maybe a mistake in the text or the code—we would be grateful if you could report this to us. By doing so, you can save other readers from frustration and help us improve subsequent versions of this book. If you find any errata, please report them by visiting http://www.packtpub.com/submit-errata, selecting your book, clicking on the **Errata Submission Form** link, and entering the details of your errata. Once your errata are verified, your submission will be accepted and the errata will be uploaded to our website or added to any list of existing errata under the Errata section of that title.

To view the previously submitted errata, go to https://www.packtpub.com/books/content/support and enter the name of the book in the search field. The required information will appear under the **Errata** section.

Piracy

Piracy of copyrighted material on the Internet is an ongoing problem across all media. At Packt, we take the protection of our copyright and licenses very seriously. If you come across any illegal copies of our works in any form on the Internet, please provide us with the location address or website name immediately so that we can pursue a remedy.

Please contact us at copyright@packtpub.com with a link to the suspected pirated material.

We appreciate your help in protecting our authors and our ability to bring you valuable content.

Questions

If you have a problem with any aspect of this book, you can contact us at questions@packtpub.com, and we will do our best to address the problem.

1
Writing Your First Manifests

Over the last few years, configuration management has become increasingly significant to the IT world. Server operations in particular are hardly even feasible without a robust management infrastructure. Among the available tools, Puppet has established itself as one of the most popular and widespread solutions. Originally written by Luke Kanies, the tool is now distributed under the terms of Apache License 2.0 and maintained by Luke's company, Puppet Labs. It boasts a large and bustling community, rich APIs for plugins and supporting tools, outstanding online documentation, and a great security model based on SSL authentication.

Like all configuration management systems, Puppet allows you to maintain a central repository of infrastructure definitions, along with a toolchain to enforce the desired state on the systems under management. The whole feature set is quite impressive. This book will guide you through some steps to quickly grasp the most important aspects and principles of Puppet.

In this chapter, we will cover the following topics:

- Getting started
- Introducing resources and properties
- Interpreting the output of the `puppet apply` command
- Adding control structures in manifests
- Using variables
- Controlling the order of evaluation
- Implementing resource interaction
- Examining the most notable resource types

Getting started

Installing Puppet is easy. On large Linux distributions, you can just install the Puppet package via apt-get or yum.

> Puppet moves a lot faster than most distributions. To be more up to date, you can install current packages directly from the Puppet Labs repositories. You can visit https://docs.puppetlabs.com/guides/install_puppet/pre_install.html for more details.

A platform-independent way to install Puppet is to get the puppet Ruby gem. This is fine for testing and managing single systems, but is not recommended for production use.

After installing Puppet, you can use it to do something for you right away. Puppet is driven by manifests, the equivalent of scripts or programs, written in Puppet's **domain-specific language (DSL)**. Let's start with the obligatory *Hello world* manifest:

```
# hello_world.pp
notify {
    'Hello, world!':
}
```

Downloading the example code

You can download the example code files for all Packt books you have purchased from your account at http://www.packtpub.com. If you purchased this book elsewhere, you can visit http://www.packtpub.com/support and register to have the files e-mailed directly to you.

To put the manifest to work, use the following command. (I avoided the term "execute" on purpose—manifests cannot be executed. More details will follow around the middle of this chapter.)

```
root@puppetagent# puppet apply hello_world.pp
Notice: Compiled catalog for puppetagent.example.net in environme
nt production in 0.03 seconds
Notice: Hello, world!
Notice: /Stage[main]/Main/Notify[Hello, world!]/message: defined
'message' as 'Hello, world!'
Notice: Finished catalog run in 0.07 seconds
```

Before we take a look at the structure of the manifest and the output from the `puppet apply` command, let's do something useful, just as an example. Puppet comes with its own background service. Assume you want to learn the basics before letting it mess with your system. You can write a manifest to have Puppet make sure that the service is not currently running and will not be started at system boot:

```
# puppet_service.pp
service {
    'puppet':
        ensure => 'stopped',
        enable => false,
}
```

To control system processes, boot options, and the like, Puppet needs to be run with root privileges. This is the most common way to invoke the tool, because Puppet will often manage OS-level facilities. Apply your new manifest with root access, either through `sudo` or from a root shell, as shown in the following screenshot:

```
root@puppetagent# puppet apply puppet_service.pp
Notice: Compiled catalog for puppetagent.example.net in environme
nt production in 0.14 seconds
Notice: /Stage[main]/Main/Service[puppet]/enable: enable changed
'true' to 'false'
Notice: Finished catalog run in 0.42 seconds
```

Now, Puppet has disabled the automatic startup of its background service for you. Applying the same manifest again has no effect, because the necessary steps are already complete:

```
root@puppetagent# puppet apply puppet_service.pp
Notice: Compiled catalog for puppetagent.example.net in environme
nt production in 0.15 seconds
Notice: Finished catalog run in 0.27 seconds
```

You will often get this output from Puppet. It tells you that everything is as it should be. As such, this is a desirable outcome, like the `all clean` output from `git status`.

> If you are following along, you might get a different output depending on your version of Puppet. All examples in this book use the 3.6.2 release from Puppet Labs' repository.

Introducing resources and properties

Each of the manifests you wrote in the previous section declared one respective resource. Resources are the elementary building blocks of manifests. Each has a type (in this case, `notify` and `service`, respectively) and a name or title (`Hello, world!` and `puppet`). Each resource is unique to a manifest and can be referenced by the combination of its type and name, such as `Service["puppet"]`. Finally, a resource also comprises a list of zero or more attributes. An attribute is a key-value pair such as `"enable => false"`.

Attribute names cannot be chosen arbitrarily. Each resource type supports a specific set of attributes. Certain parameters are available for all resource types, and some names are just very common, such as `ensure`. The service type supports the `ensure` property, which represents the status of the managed process. Its `enabled` property, on the other hand, relates to the system boot configuration (with respect to the service in question).

Note that I have used the terms attribute, property, and parameter in a seemingly interchangeable fashion. Don't be deceived — there are important distinctions. Property and parameter are the two different kinds of attributes that Puppet uses. You have already seen two properties in action. Let's look at a parameter:

```
service {
    'puppet':
        ensure   => 'stopped',
        enable   => false,
        provider => 'upstart',
}
```

The `provider` parameter tells Puppet that it needs to interact with the `upstart` subsystem to control its background service, as opposed to `systemd` or `init`. If you don't specify this parameter, Puppet makes a well-educated guess. There is quite a multitude of supported facilities to manage services on a system. You will learn more about providers and their automatic choosing later.

The difference between parameters and properties is that the parameter merely indicates *how* Puppet should manage the resource, not what a desired state is. Puppet will only take action on property values. In this example, these are `ensure => 'stopped'` and `enable => false`. For each such property, it will perform the following tasks:

- Test whether the resource is already in sync with the target state
- If the resource is not in sync, trigger a sync action

A property is considered to be in sync when the system entity that is managed by the given resource (in this case, the upstart service configuration for Puppet) is in the state that is described by the property value in the manifest. In this example, the ensure property will be in sync only if the puppet service is not running. The enable property is in sync if upstart is not configured to launch Puppet at system start.

As a mnemonic concerning parameters versus properties, just remember that properties can be out of sync, whereas parameters cannot.

Interpreting the output of the puppet apply command

As you have already witnessed, the output presented by Puppet is rather verbose. As you get more experienced with the tool, you will quickly learn to spot the crucial pieces of information. Let's first look at the informational messages though. Apply the service.pp manifest once more:

```
root@puppetagent# puppet apply puppet_service.pp
Notice: Compiled catalog for puppetagent.example.net in environme
nt production in 0.15 seconds
Notice: Finished catalog run in 0.27 seconds
```

Puppet took no particular action. You only get two timings—one from the compiling phase of the manifest and the other from the catalog application phase. The catalog is a comprehensive representation of a compiled manifest. Puppet bases all its efforts concerning the evaluation and syncing of resources on the content of its current catalog.

Now, to quickly force Puppet to show you some more interesting output, pass it a one-line manifest directly from the shell. Regular users of Ruby or Perl will recognize the call syntax:

```
root@puppetagent# puppet apply -e 'service { "puppet": enable =>
true }'
Notice: Compiled catalog for puppetagent.example.net in environme
nt production in 0.14 seconds
Notice: /Stage[main]/Main/Service[puppet]/enable: enable changed
'false' to 'true'
Notice: Finished catalog run in 0.49 seconds
```

I prefer double quotes in manifests that get passed as command-line arguments, because on the shell, the manifest should be enclosed in single quotes as a whole, if at least for convenience.

You instructed Puppet to perform yet another change upon the Puppet service. The output reflects the exact change that is performed. Let's analyze this log message:

- The `Notice:` keyword at the beginning of the line represents the log level. Other levels include `Warning`, `Error`, and `Debug`.

- The property that changed is referenced with a whole path, starting with `Stage[main]`. Stages are beyond the scope of this book, so you will always just see the default of `main` here.

- The next path element is `Main`, which is another default. It denotes the class in which the resource was declared. You will learn about classes in *Chapter 4, Modularizing Manifests with Classes and Defined Types*.

- Next is the resource. You already learned that `Service[puppet]` is its unique reference.

- Finally, `enable` is the name of the property in question. When several properties are out of sync, there will usually be one line of output for each property that gets synchronized.

- The rest of the log line indicates the type of change that Puppet saw fit to apply. The wording depends on the nature of the property. It can be as simple as `created` for a resource that is newly added to the managed system, or a short phrase such as `changed false to true`.

Dry-testing your manifest

Another useful command-line switch for `puppet apply` is the `--noop` option. It instructs Puppet to refrain from taking any action on unsynced resources. Instead, you only get log output that indicates what will change without the switch. This is useful to determine whether a manifest would possibly break anything on your system:

```
root@puppetagent# puppet apply puppet_service.pp --noop
Notice: Compiled catalog for puppetagent.example.net in environme
nt production in 0.14 seconds
Notice: /Stage[main]/Main/Service[puppet]/enable: current_value t
rue, should be false (noop)
Notice: Class[Main]: Would have triggered 'refresh' from 1 events
Notice: Stage[main]: Would have triggered 'refresh' from 1 events
Notice: Finished catalog run in 0.23 seconds
```

Note that the output format is the same as before, with a (noop) marker trailing the notice about the sync action. This log can be considered a preview of what will happen when the manifest is applied.

The additional notices about triggered refreshes are usually not important and can be ignored. You will have a better understanding of their significance after finishing this chapter and *Chapter 4, Modularizing Manifests with Classes and Defined Types*.

Adding control structures in manifests

You have written three simple manifests while following along with this chapter so far. Each comprised only one resource, and one of them was given on the command line using the -e option. Of course, you would not want to write distinct manifests for each possible circumstance. Instead, just as how Ruby or Perl scripts branch out into different code paths, there are structures that make your Puppet code flexible and reusable for different circumstances.

The most common control element is the if/else block. It is quite similar to its equivalent in many programming languages:

```
if 'mail_lda' in $needed_services {
    service { 'dovecot': enable => true }
} else {
    service { 'dovecot': enable => false }
}
```

The Puppet DSL also has a case statement, which is reminiscent of its counterpart in other languages as well:

```
case $role {
    'imap_server': {
        package { 'dovecot': ensure => 'installed' }
        service { 'dovecot': ensure => 'running' }
    }
    /_webserver$/: {
        service { [ 'apache', 'ssh' ]: ensure => 'running' }
    }
    default: {
        service { 'ssh': ensure => running }
    }
}
```

A variation of the case statement is the selector. It's an expression, not a statement, and can be used in a fashion similar to the ternary if/else operator found in C-like languages:

```
package {
    'dovecot': ensure => $role ? {
```

```
            'imap_server' => 'installed',
            /desktop$/    => 'purged',
            default       => 'removed',
        }
    }
```

In more complex manifests, this syntax will impede readability. Puppet Labs recommend to use it only in variable assignments.

Using variables

Variable assignment works just like in most scripting languages. Any variable name is always prefixed with the $ sign:

```
$download_server = 'img2.example.net'
$url = "https://${download_server}/pkg/example_source.tar.gz"
```

Also, just like most scripting languages, Puppet performs variable value substitution in strings that are in double quotes, but no interpolation at all in single-quoted strings.

Variables are useful to make your manifest more concise and comprehensible. They help you with the overall goal of keeping your source code free from redundancy. An important distinction from variables in imperative programming and scripting languages is the **immutability** of variables in Puppet manifests. Once a value has been assigned, it cannot be overwritten.

Under specific circumstances, it is possible to amend values through concatenation. You might encounter statements such as for $variable += 'value'. This should be used with care, or avoided altogether.

Variable types

As of Puppet 3.x, there are only three variable types: strings, arrays, and hashes. Puppet 4 introduces a rich type system, but this is out of the scope of this book. The three variable types work much like their respective counterparts in other languages. Depending on your background, you might be familiar with associative arrays or dictionaries as semantic equivalents to Puppet's hash type:

```
$a_string = 'This is a string value'
$an_array = [ 'This', 'forms', 'an', 'array' ]
$a_hash   = {
    'subject'   => 'Hashes',
```

```
              'predicate' => 'are written',
              'object'    => 'like this',
              'note'      => 'not actual grammar!',
              'also note' => [ 'nesting is',
                              { 'allowed' => 'of course' } ],
    }
```

Accessing the values is equally simple. Note that the hash syntax is similar to that of Ruby, not Perl's:

```
$x = $a_string
$y = $an_array[1]
$z = $a_hash['object']
```

Strings can obviously be used as resource attribute values, but it's worth noting that a resource title can also be a variable reference:

```
package {
    $apache_package:
        ensure => 'installed'
}
```

It's intuitively clear what a string value means in this context. But you can also pass arrays here to declare a whole set of resources in one statement. The following manifest manages three packages, making sure that they are all installed:

```
$packages = [ 'apache2',
              'libapache2-mod-php5',
              'libapache2-mod-passenger', ]
package {
    $packages:
        ensure => 'installed'
}
```

You will learn how to make efficient use of hash values in later chapters.

 The array does not *need* to be stored in a variable to be used this way, but it is a good practice in some cases.

Controlling the order of evaluation

With what you've seen thus far, you might have gotten the impression that Puppet's DSL is a specialized scripting language. That is actually quite far from the truth—a manifest is not a script or program. The language is a tool to model a system state through a set of software resources, including files, packages, and cron jobs, among others.

The whole paradigm is different from that of scripting languages. Whereas Ruby or Perl are imperative languages, which are based around statements that will be evaluated in a strict order, the Puppet DSL is declarative: the manifest declares a set of resources that are expected to have certain properties.

In other words, the manifests should always describe what you expect to be the end result. The specifics of what actions need to be taken to get there are decided by Puppet.

To make this distinction more clear, let's look at an example:

```
package {
    'haproxy': ensure => 'installed',
}
file {
    '/etc/haproxy/haproxy.cfg':
        owner  => 'root',
        group  => 'root',
        mode   => '644',
        source =>
            'puppet:///modules/haproxy/etc/haproxy/haproxy.cfg',
}
service {
    'haproxy': ensure => 'running',
}
```

The manifest has Puppet make sure that:

- The HAproxy package is installed
- The haproxy.cfg file has specific content, which has been prepared in a file in /etc/puppet/modules/
- HAproxy is started

To make this work, it is important that the necessary steps are performed in order. A configuration file cannot usually be installed before the package, because there is not yet a directory to contain it. The service cannot start before installation either. If it becomes active before the configuration is in place, it will use the default settings from the package instead.

This point is being stressed because the preceding manifest does not, in fact, contain cues for Puppet to indicate such a strict ordering. Without explicit dependencies, Puppet is free to put the resources in any order it sees fit.

 The recent versions of Puppet allow a form of local manifest-based ordering, so the presented example will actually work as is. It is still important to be aware of the ordering principles, because the implicit order is difficult to determine in more complex manifests, and as you will learn soon, there are other factors that will influence the order.

Declaring dependencies

The easiest way to bring order to such a straightforward manifest is **resource chaining**. The syntax for that is a simple ASCII arrow between two resources:

```
package {
    'haproxy': ensure => 'installed',
}
->
file {
    '/etc/haproxy/haproxy.cfg':
        owner  => 'root',
        group  => 'root',
        mode   => '644',
        source => 'puppet:///modules/haproxy/etc/haproxy/haproxy.cfg',
}
->
service {
    'haproxy': ensure => 'running',
}
```

This is only viable if all the related resources can be written next to each other. In other words, if the graphic representation of the dependencies does not form a straight chain, but more of a tree, star, or other shape, this syntax is not sufficient.

 Internally, Puppet *will* construct an ordered graph of resources and synchronize them during a traversal of that graph.

A more generic and flexible way to declare dependencies are specialized **metaparameters** — parameters that are eligible for use with any resource type. There are different metaparameters, most of which have nothing to do with ordering (you have seen `provider` in an earlier example), but for now, let's concentrate on `require` and `before`. Here is the `HAproxy` manifest, ordered using the `require` metaparameter:

```
package {
    'haproxy': ensure => 'installed',
}
file {
    '/etc/haproxy/haproxy.cfg':
        owner   => 'root',
        group   => 'root',
        mode    => '644',
        source  =>
            'puppet:///modules/haproxy/etc/haproxy/haproxy.cfg',
        require => Package['haproxy'],
}
service {
    'haproxy':
        ensure  => 'running',
        require => File['/etc/haproxy/haproxy.cfg'],
}
```

The following manifest is semantically identical, but relies on the `before` metaparameter rather than `require`:

```
package {
    'haproxy':
        ensure => 'installed',
        before => File['/etc/haproxy/haproxy.cfg'],
}
file {
    '/etc/haproxy/haproxy.cfg':
        owner  => 'root',
        group  => 'root',
        mode   => '644',
        source =>
            'puppet:///modules/haproxy/etc/haproxy/haproxy.cfg',
        before => Service['haproxy'],
}
service {
    'haproxy': ensure => 'running',
}
```

The manifest can also mix both styles of notation, of course. This is left as a reader exercise with no dedicated depiction.

The `require` metaparameter usually leads to more understandable code, because it expresses a dependency of the annotated resource on another resource. The `before` parameter, on the other hand, implies a dependency that a referenced resource forms upon the current resource. This can be counter-intuitive, especially for frequent users of packaging systems (which usually implement a `require` style dependency declaration).

The `before` metaparameter is still outright necessary in certain situations and can make the manifest code more elegant and straightforward for others. Familiarity with both variants is advisable.

Let's see an example of dependencies that do not form a straight chain. In the following code, Puppet manages the configuration directory explicitly, so the config file can be deployed independently of the package. The service's requirements are passed in an array:

```
package {
    'haproxy': ensure => 'installed',
}
file {
    '/etc/haproxy':
        ensure => 'directory',
        owner  => 'root',
        group  => 'root',
        mode   => '644';
    '/etc/haproxy/haproxy.cfg':
        owner  => 'root',
        group  => 'root',
        mode   => '644',
        source =>
            'puppet:///modules/haproxy/etc/haproxy/haproxy.cfg',
}
service {
    'haproxy':
        ensure => 'running',
        require => [
            File['/etc/haproxy/haproxy.cfg'],
            Package['haproxy'],
        ],
}
```

Puppet will automatically make the config file require the containing directory if it is part of your manifest. There is no need to add the metaparameter explicitly. This is a special function of `file` resources.

The manifest saves lines by declaring both `file` resources in one block, separated by a semicolon.

Error propagation

Defining requirements serves another important purpose. I have used the term **dependency** in this context before. This wording was deliberate—aside from defining a mandatory order of evaluation, the `require` and `before` parameters bond the involved resources into a unidirectional failure pair. For example, a `file` resource will fail if the URL of the `source` file is broken:

```
file {
    '/etc/haproxy/haproxy.cfg':
        source => 'puppet:///modules/haproxy/etc/haproxy.cfg'
}
```

Puppet will report that the resource could not be synchronized:

```
root@agent# puppet apply typo.pp
Notice: Compiled catalog for agent.example.net in environment pro
duction in 0.25 seconds
Error: /Stage[main]/Main/File[/etc/haproxy/haproxy.cfg]: Could no
t evaluate: Could not retrieve information from environment produ
ction source(s) puppet:///modules/haproxy/etc/haproxy.cfg
Notice: /Stage[main]/Main/Service[haproxy]: Dependency File[/etc/
haproxy/haproxy.cfg] has failures: true
Warning: /Stage[main]/Main/Service[haproxy]: Skipping because of
failed dependencies
Notice: Finished catalog run in 0.13 seconds
```

In this screenshot, the `Error` line describes the error caused by the broken URL. The error propagation is represented by the `Notice` and `Warning` keywords below that.

Puppet failed to apply changes to the configuration file—it cannot compare the current state to the nonexistent source. As the service depends on the configuration file, Puppet will not even try to start it. This is for safety: if any dependencies cannot be put into the defined state, Puppet must assume that the system is not fit for application of the dependent resource.

This is another important reason to make consequent use of resource dependencies. Remember that the chaining arrow and the `before` metaparameter imply the same semantics.

Avoiding circular dependencies

Before you learn about another way in which resources can interrelate, there is an issue that you should be aware of: dependencies must not form circles. Let's visualize this in an example:

```
file {
    '/etc/haproxy':
        ensure => 'directory',
        owner  => 'root',
        group  => 'root',
        mode   => '644';
    '/etc/haproxy/haproxy.cfg':
        owner  => 'root',
        group  => 'root',
        mode   => '644',
        source =>
            'puppet:///modules/haproxy/etc/haproxy/haproxy.cfg',
}
service {
    'haproxy':
        ensure  => 'running',
        require => File['/etc/haproxy/haproxy.cfg'],
        before  => File['/etc/haproxy'],
}
```

The dependency circle in this manifest is somewhat hidden (as will likely be the case for many such circles that you will encounter during regular use of Puppet). It is formed by the following relations:

- The `File['/etc/haproxy/haproxy.cfg']` autorequires the parent directory, `File['/etc/haproxy']`
- The parent directory, `File['/etc/haproxy']`, requires `Service['haproxy']`, due to the latter's `before` metaparameter
- The `Service['haproxy']` requires the `File['/etc/haproxy/haproxy.cfg']` config

Granted, the example is contrived—it will not make sense to manage the service before the configuration directory. Nevertheless, even a manifest design that is apparently sound can result in circular dependencies. This is how Puppet will react to that:

```
root@puppetagent# puppet apply circle.pp
Notice: Compiled catalog for puppetagent.example.net in environme
nt production in 0.25 seconds
Error: Could not apply complete catalog: Found 1 dependency cycle
:
(File[/etc/haproxy/haproxy.cfg] => Service[haproxy] => File[/etc/
haproxy] => File[/etc/haproxy/haproxy.cfg])
Try the '--graph' option and opening the resulting '.dot' file in
 OmniGraffle or GraphViz
Notice: Finished catalog run in 0.06 seconds
```

The output helps you to locate the offending relation(s). For very wide dependency circles with lots of involved resources, the textual rendering is difficult to analyze. Therefore, Puppet also gives you the opportunity to get a graphical representation of the dependency graph through the `--graph` option.

If you do this, Puppet will include the full path to the newly created `.dot` file in its output. Its content looks similar to Puppet's output:

```
digraph Resource_Cycles {
  label = "Resource Cycles"
"File[/etc/haproxy/haproxy.cfg]" -> "Service[haproxy]" -> "File[/etc/
haproxy]" -> "File[/etc/haproxy/haproxy.cfg]"
}
```

This is not helpful by itself, but it can be fed directly to tools such as `dotty` to produce an actual diagram.

To summarize, resource dependencies are helpful in order to keep Puppet from acting upon resources in unexpected or uncontrolled situations. They are also useful to restrict the order of resource evaluation.

Implementing resource interaction

In addition to dependencies, resources can also enter a similar but different mutual relation. Remember the pieces of output that we skipped earlier:

```
root@puppetagent# puppet apply puppet_service.pp --noop
Notice: Compiled catalog for puppetagent.example.net in environme
nt production in 0.14 seconds
Notice: /Stage[main]/Main/Service[puppet]/enable: current_value t
rue, should be false (noop)
Notice: Class[Main]: Would have triggered 'refresh' from 1 events
Notice: Stage[main]: Would have triggered 'refresh' from 1 events
Notice: Finished catalog run in 0.23 seconds
```

Puppet mentions that **refreshes** would have been triggered for the reason of an **event**. Such events are emitted by resources whenever Puppet acts on the need for a sync action. Without explicit code to receive and react to events, they just get discarded.

The mechanism to set up such event receivers is named in analogy to a generic publish/subscribe queue—resources get configured to react to events using the subscribe metaparameter. There is no publish keyword or parameter, since each and every resource is technically a publisher of events (messages). Instead, the counterpart of the subscribe metaparameter is called notify, and it explicitly directs generated events at referenced resources.

One of the most common practical uses of the event system is the ability to reload service configurations. When a service resource consumes an event (usually from a change in a config file), Puppet invokes the appropriate action to make the service restart.

 If you instruct Puppet to do this, it can result in brief service interruptions due to this restart operation. Note that if the new configuration causes an error, the service might fail to start and stay offline.

```
file {
    '/etc/haproxy/haproxy.cfg':
        owner   => 'root',
        group   => 'root',
        mode    => '644',
        source  =>
            'puppet:///modules/haproxy/etc/haproxy/haproxy.cfg',
        require => Package['haproxy'],
}
service {
    'haproxy':
        ensure    => 'running',
        subscribe => File['/etc/haproxy/haproxy.cfg'],
}
```

If the `notify` metaparameter is to be used instead, it must be specified for the resource that emits the event:

```
file {
    '/etc/haproxy/haproxy.cfg':
        owner   => 'root',
        group   => 'root',
        mode    => '644',
        source  =>
            'puppet:///modules/haproxy/etc/haproxy/haproxy.cfg',
        require => Package['haproxy'],
        notify  => Service['haproxy'],
}
service {
    'haproxy': ensure  => 'running',
}
```

This will likely feel reminiscent of the `before` and `subscribe` metaparameters, which offer symmetric ways of expressing an interrelation of a pair of resources just as well. This is not a coincidence — these metaparameters are closely related to each other:

- The resource that subscribes to another resource implicitly requires it
- The resource that notifies another is implicitly placed before the latter one in the dependency graph

In other words, `subscribe` is the same as `require`, except for the dependent resource receiving events from its peer. The same holds true for `notify` and `before`.

The chaining syntax is also available for signaling. To establish a signaling relation between neighboring resources, use an ASCII arrow with a tilde, `~>`, instead of the dash in `->`:

```
file { '/etc/haproxy/haproxy.cfg': … }
~>
service { 'haproxy': … }
```

The `service` resource type is one of the two notable types that support **refreshing** when resources get notified (the other will be discussed in the next section). There are others, but they are not as ubiquitous.

Examining the most notable resource types

To complete our tour of the basic elements of a manifest, let's take a closer look at the resource types you have already used and some of the more important ones that you have not yet encountered.

You probably already have a good feeling for the `file` type, which will ensure the existence of files and directories, along with their permissions. Pulling a file from a repository (usually, a Puppet module) is also a frequent use case, using the `source` parameter. For very short files, it is more economic to include the desired content right in the manifest:

```
file {
    '/etc/modules':
        content => "# Managed by Puppet!\n\ndrbd\n",
}
```

> The double quotes allow expansion of escape sequences such as \n.

Another useful capability is managing symbolic links:

```
file {
    '/etc/apache2/sites-enabled/001-puppet-lore.org':
        ensure => 'link',
        target => '../sites-available/puppet-lore.org';
    '/etc/apache2/sites-enabled/002-wordpress':
        ensure => '../sites-available/wordpress',
}
```

Using the link target as the `ensure` value is possible but not recommended.

The next type you already know is `package`, and its typical usage is quite intuitive. Make sure that packages are either installed or removed. A notable use case you have not yet seen is to use the basic package manager instead of `apt` or `yum`/`zypper`. This is useful if the package is not available from a repository:

```
package {
    'haproxy':
        provider => 'dpkg',
        source   => '/opt/packages/haproxy-1.5.1_amd64.dpkg',
}
```

> Your mileage usually increases if you make the effort of setting
> up a simple repository instead so that the main package manager
> can be used after all.

Last but not least, there is the `service` type, the most important attributes of which
you already know as well. It's worth pointing out that it can serve as a simple
shortcut in cases where you don't wish to add a full-fledged `init` script or similar.
With enough information, the `base` provider for the `service` type will manage
simple background processes for you:

```
service {
    'count-logins':
        provider  => 'base',
        ensure    => 'running',
        binary    => '/usr/local/bin/cnt-logins',
        start     => '/usr/local/bin/cnt-logins --daemonize',
        subscribe => File['/usr/local/bin/cnt-logins'],
}
```

Puppet will not only restart the script if it is not running for some reason, but also
will restart it whenever the content changes. This only works if Puppet manages
the file content and all changes propagate through Puppet only.

> If Puppet changes any other property of the script file (for example,
> the `file` mode), that too will lead to a restart of the process.

Let's look at some other types you will probably need.

The user and group types

Especially in the absence of central registries such as LDAP, it is useful to be able
to manage user accounts on each of your machines. There are providers for all
supported platforms; however, the available attributes vary. On Linux, the `useradd`
provider is the most common. It allows the management of all fields in `/etc/passwd`,
such as `uid` and `shell`, but also group memberships:

```
group {
    'proxy-admins':
        ensure => present,
        gid    => 4002,
}
```

```
user {
    'john':
        uid        => 2014,
        home       => '/home/john'
        managehome => true, # <- adds -m to useradd
        gid        => 1000,
        shell      => '/bin/zsh',
        groups     => [ 'proxy-admins' ],
}
```

As with all resources, Puppet will not only make sure that the user and group exist, but also fix any divergent properties such as the home directory.

Even though the user depends on the group, because it cannot be added before the group exists, this need not be expressed in the manifest. The user automatically requires all necessary groups, similar to file autorequiring its parent directory.

Note that Puppet will also happily manage your LDAP user accounts.

The exec resource type

There is one oddball resource type in the Puppet core. Remember my earlier assertion that Puppet is not a specialized scripting engine, but instead a tool that allows you to model part of your system state in a compelling DSL and is capable of altering your system to meet the defined goal. This is why you declare a user and a group, for example, instead of invoking groupadd and useradd in order. You can do this because Puppet comes with support to manage such entities. This is vastly beneficial, because Puppet also knows that on different platforms, other commands are used for account management and that the arguments can be subtly different on some systems.

Of course, Puppet does not have knowledge of all conceivable particulars of any supported system. Say you wish to manage an OpenAFS file server—there are no specific resource types to aid you with this. The ideal solution is to exploit Puppet's plugin system and to write your own types and providers so that your manifests can just reflect the AFS-specific configuration. This is not simple though and also not worthwhile in cases where you only need Puppet to invoke some exotic commands from very few places in your manifest.

For such cases, Puppet ships with the `exec` resource type, which allows the execution of custom commands in lieu of an abstract sync action. For example, it can be used to unpack a tarball in the absence of a proper package:

```
exec {
    'tar cjf /opt/packages/homebrewn-3.2.tar.bz2':
        cwd     => '/opt',
        path    => '/bin:/usr/bin',
        creates => '/opt/homebrewn-3.2',
}
```

The `creates` parameter is important for Puppet to tell whether the command needs running—once the specified path exists, the resource counts as synced. For commands that do not create a telltale file or directory, there are alternative parameters, `onlyif` and `unless`, to allow Puppet to query the sync state:

```
exec {
    'perl -MCPAN -e "install YAML"':
        path   => '/bin:/usr/bin',
        unless => 'cpan -l | grep -qP ^YAML\\b'
}
```

The query command's exit code determines the state. In the case of `unless`, the `exec` command runs if the query fails.

Finally, the `exec` type resources are the second notable case of receivers for events using `notify` and `subscribe`:

```
exec {
    'apt-get update':
        path          => '/bin:/usr/bin',
        subscribe     =>
            File['/etc/apt/sources.list.d/jenkins.list'],
        refreshonly => true,
}
```

You can even chain multiple `exec` resources in this fashion so that each invocation triggers the next one. However, this is a bad practice and degrades Puppet to a (rather flawed) scripting engine. The `exec` resources should be avoided in favor of regular resources whenever possible. Some resource types that are not part of the core are available as plugins from the Puppet Forge. You will learn more about this topic in *Chapter 5, Extending Your Puppet Infrastructure with Modules*.

Since `exec` resources can be used to perform virtually *any* operation, they are sometimes abused to stand in for more proper resource types. This is a typical antipattern in Puppet manifests. It is safer to regard `exec` resources as the last resort, which are only to be used if all other alternatives have been exhausted.

Let's briefly discuss two more types that are supported out of the box. They allow the management of cron jobs and mounted partitions and shares, respectively, which are frequent requirements in server operation.

The cron resource type

A cron job mainly consists of a command and the recurring time and date at which to run the command. Puppet models the command and each date particle as a property of a resource with the cron type:

```
cron {
    'clean-files':
        ensure      => present,
        user        => 'root',
        command     => '/usr/local/bin/clean-files',
        minute      => '1',
        hour        => '3',
        weekday     => [ '2', '6' ],
        environment => 'MAILTO=felix@example.net',
}
```

The environment property allows you to specify one or more variable bindings for cron to add to the job.

The mount resource type

Finally, Puppet will manage all aspects about mountable filesystems for you—their basic attributes such as the source device and mount point, the mount options, and the current state. A line from the fstab file translates quite literally to a Puppet manifest:

```
mount {
    '/media/gluster-data':
        ensure  => 'mounted',
        device  => 'gluster01:/data',
        fstype  => 'glusterfs',
        options => 'defaults,_netdev',
        dump    => 0,
        pass    => 0,
}
```

For this resource, Puppet will make sure that the filesystem is indeed mounted after the run. Ensuring the unmounted state is also possible, of course, but Puppet can also just make sure the entry is present in the fstab file, or absent from the system altogether.

Summary

After installing Puppet on your system, you can use it by writing and applying manifests. These are programs that are written in Puppet's DSL. Even though they resemble scripts, they should not be considered as such. For one thing, they consist of resources instead of commands. These resources are generally not evaluated in the order in which they have been written. An explicit ordering should be defined through the require and before metaparameters instead.

Each resource has a number of attributes: parameters and properties. Each property is evaluated in its own right; Puppet detects whether a change to the system is necessary to get any property into the state that is defined in the manifest. It will also perform such changes. This is referred to as **synchronizing** a resource or property.

The ordering parameters, require and before, are of further importance because they establish dependency of one resource upon one or more others. This allows Puppet to skip parts of the manifest if an important resource cannot be synchronized. Circular dependencies must be avoided.

Each resource in the manifest has a resource type that describes the nature of the system entity that is being managed. Some of the types that are used most frequently are file, package, and service. Puppet comes with many types for convenient system management, and many plugins are available to add even more. Some tasks require the use of exec resources, but this should be done sparingly.

In the next chapter, we will have a look at the master/agent setup.

2
The Master and Its Agents

So far, you have dealt with some concise Puppet manifests that were built to model some very specific goals. By means of the `puppet apply` command, you can use such snippets on any machine in your infrastructure. This is not the most common way of using Puppet, though, and this chapter will introduce you to the popular master/agent structure. It's worth noting, however, that applying standalone manifests can always be useful, independent of your overall Puppet design.

Under the master/agent paradigm, you will typically install the Puppet agent software on all nodes under your care and make them call in to the master, which is yet another Puppet installation. The master will compile appropriate manifests and effectively remotely control the agents. Both the agent and the master authenticate themselves using trusted SSL certificates.

This chapter covers the following topics:

- The Puppet master
- Setting up the Puppet agent
- Performance considerations
- SSL troubleshooting

The Puppet master

Many Puppet-based workflows are centered around the master, which is a central source of configuration data and authority. The master hands instructions to all computer systems in the infrastructure (where agents are installed). It serves multiple purposes in the distributed system of Puppet components.

The master will perform the following tasks:

- Storing and compiling manifests
- Serving as the SSL certification authority
- Processing reports from the agent machines
- Gathering and storing information about the agents

As such, the security of your master machine is paramount, which is not unlike a Kerberos Key Distribution Center.

During its first initialization, the Puppet master generates the CA certificate. This self-signed certificate will be distributed among and trusted by all pieces of your infrastructure. This is why its private key must be protected very carefully. New agent machines request individual certificates, which are signed with the CA certificate.

 It's a good idea to include a copy of the CA certificate in your OS-provisioning process so that the agent can establish the authenticity of the master before requesting its individual certificate.

Setting up the master machine

The software that implements the basic master functionality is identical to the Puppet package that you installed during the first chapter; remember how you invoked it as `puppet apply` at the time? Like several source control software (such as `git`), the puppet CLI tool implements various subcommands that can perform very different tasks. You can basically start a Puppet master on any machine by running `puppet master`.

This is obviously not an acceptable mode of running an essential service. For a durable production setup, there is a specialized package of scripts and wrappers called `puppetmaster`.

 Puppet Labs' online documentation has detailed step-by-step information on how to prepare your system for the installation of their packages at `https://docs.puppetlabs.com/guides/install_puppet/pre_install.html`.

Once this package is installed, you should be able to control the master operation via the puppetmaster system service. In fact, the master service starts up and initializes itself with the default settings right after the package installation. This might not fit your requirements yet, but let's keep these defaults for the moment.

Creating the master manifest

When you used Puppet locally during *Chapter 1*, *Writing Your First Manifests*, you specified a manifest file that puppet apply should compile. The master compiles manifests for many machines, but the agent does not get to choose which source file is to be used—this is fully at the master's discretion. The starting point for any compilation by the master is always the **site manifest**, which can be found at /etc/puppet/manifests/site.pp.

 The path is configurable, of course.

Each connecting agent will use the manifest found there. Of course, you don't want to manage only one identical set of resources on all of your machines. To define a piece of manifest exclusively for a specific agent, put it in a node block. This block's contents will only be considered when the calling agent has a matching common name in its SSL certificate. You can dedicate a piece of manifest to a machine with the name of agent, for example:

```
node 'agent' {
    $packages = [ 'apache2',
        'libapache2-mod-php5',
        'libapache2-mod-passenger', ]
    package {
        $packages:
            ensure => 'installed',
    }
    ->
    service {
        'apache2':
            ensure => 'running',
            enable => true,
    }
}
```

Before you set up and connect your first agent to the master, step back and think about how the master should be addressed. By default, agents will try to resolve the unqualified `puppet` hostname in order to get the master's address. If you have a default domain that gets searched by your machines, you can use this default and add a record for `puppet` as a subdomain. Otherwise, pick a domain name that seems fitting to you, such as `master.example.net` or `adm01.example.net`. What's important is that:

- All your agent machines can resolve the name to an address
- The master process is listening for connections on that address
- The master uses a certificate with the chosen name as CN or SAN

The mode of resolution depends on your circumstances — the `hosts` file on each machine is one ubiquitous possibility. Puppet listens on all available addresses by default.

This leaves the task of creating a suitable certificate, which is simple. Configure the master to use the appropriate certificate name, and restart the service. If the certificate does not exist yet, Puppet will take the necessary steps to create it. Put the following setting into your `/etc/puppet/puppet.conf` file on the master machine:

```
[master]
certname=master.example.net
```

Upon its next start, the master will use the appropriate certificate for all SSL connections. The automatic proliferation of SSL data is not dangerous even in an existing setup, except for the certification authority. If the master were to generate a new CA certificate at any point in time, it would break the trust of all existing agents.

This was not obvious, but during the installation and initialization of the `puppetmaster` package, Puppet had already created a set of certificates — one for its own service, based on what the master considered its default name in your environment and the CA certificate to sign it.

 Make very sure that the data in `/var/lib/puppet/ssl/ca/` is neither lost nor compromised. All previously signed certificates become obsolete whenever Puppet needs to create a new certification authority.

Inspecting the configuration settings

All customization of the master's parameters can be made in the `puppet.conf` file. The operating system packages ship with some settings deemed sensible by the respective maintainers. Apart from these explicit settings, Puppet relies on defaults that are either built in or derived from the environment (details on how this works follow in the next chapter).

Most users will want to rely on these defaults for as many settings as possible. This is possible without any drawbacks, because Puppet makes all settings fully transparent using the `--configprint` parameter. For example, you can find out where the master manifest file is located:

```
root@puppetmaster# puppet master --configprint manifest
/etc/puppet/manifests/site.pp
```

To get an overview of all available settings and their values, use the following command:

```
root@puppetmaster# puppet master --configprint all | less
```

While this command is especially useful on the master side, the same introspection is available for `puppet apply` and `puppet agent`.

Setting up the Puppet agent

As was explained earlier, the master mainly serves instructions to agents in the form of catalogs that are compiled from the manifest. You have also prepared a `node` block for your first agent in the master manifest.

Installing the agent software is easy—you did this at the start of *Chapter 1, Writing Your First Manifests*. The plain Puppet package that allows you to apply a local manifest contains all the required parts in order to operate a proper agent.

For the initial test, the following invocation is sufficient:

```
root@agent# puppet agent --test
Info: Creating a new SSL key for agent
Error: Could not request certificate: getaddrinfo: Name or servic
e not known
Exiting; failed to retrieve certificate and waitforcert is disabl
ed
```

Puppet first created a new SSL certificate key for itself. For its own name, it picked `agent`, which is the machine's hostname. That's fine for now. An error happened, because the name `puppet` cannot be currently resolved to anything. Add it to `/etc/hosts` so that Puppet can contact the master.

```
root@agent# puppet agent --test
Info: Caching certificate for ca
Info: csr_attributes file loading from /etc/puppet/csr_attributes
.yaml
Info: Creating a new SSL certificate request for agent
Info: Certificate Request fingerprint (SHA256): FE:A0:2C:BE:FC:A7
:7A:8D:0D:E0:D9:52:05:58:A7:2D:4F:84:BE:11:3F:F2:DF:4D:F1:5D:79:1
2:9E:6F:CD:07
Info: Caching certificate for ca
Exiting; no certificate found and waitforcert is disabled
```

Note how Puppet conveniently downloaded and cached the CA certificate. The agent will establish trust based on this certificate from now on.

 This is a delicate moment during which spoofing is possible—it can be avoided by implementing a secure way to preshare the CA certificate.

Puppet created a certificate request and sent it to the master. It then immediately tried to download the signed certificate. This is expected to fail—the master won't just sign a certificate for any request it receives. This behavior is important for proper security.

 There is a configuration setting that enables such automatic signing, but users are generally discouraged from using it because it allows for the creation of arbitrary numbers of signed (and therefore, trusted) certificates to any user who has network access to the master.

To authorize the agent, look for the CSR on the master using the `puppet cert` command:

```
root@puppetmaster# puppet cert --list
  "agent" (SHA256) C9:66:45:40:67:42:ED:2D:A2:50:A4:6C:49:62:57:D1: A0:77
:B0:E4:03:CF:63:A2:96:F6:55:7D:07:23:FE:2C
```

This looks alright, so now you can sign a new certificate for the agent:

```
root@puppetmaster# puppet cert --sign agent
Notice: Signed certificate request for agent
Notice: Removing file Puppet::SSL::CertificateRequest agent at '/var/
lib/puppet/ssl/ca/requests/agent.pem'
```

When choosing mode of operation for puppet cert, the dashes in front of the option name can be omitted — you can just use puppet cert list and puppet cert sign.

Now the agent can receive its certificate for its catalog run:

```
root@agent# puppet agent --test
Info: Caching certificate for agent
Error: Could not request certificate: Server hostname 'puppet' di
d not match server certificate; expected master.example.net
Exiting; failed to retrieve certificate and waitforcert is disabl
ed
```

That didn't work. Remember that you picked a full domain name for your master earlier. The default of puppet will, therefore, not work for authenticated SSL connections. To make Puppet use the correct name, add the --server option.

```
root@agent# puppet agent --test --server=master.example.net
Info: Caching certificate for agent
Info: Caching certificate_revocation_list for ca
Info: Caching certificate for agent
Info: Retrieving pluginfacts
Info: Retrieving plugin
Info: Caching catalog for agent
Info: Applying configuration version '1411763995'
Notice: /Stage[main]/Main/Node[agent]/Package[libapache2-mod-php5
]/ensure: created
Notice: /Stage[main]/Main/Node[agent]/Package[apache2]/ensure: en
sure changed 'purged' to 'present'
Notice: /Stage[main]/Main/Node[agent]/Package[libapache2-mod-pass
enger]/ensure: created
Notice: Finished catalog run in 16.43 seconds
```

This output indicates a successful agent run. The manifest inside the node block from site.pp on the master was used — the node name, which is agent, matches the certificate of the new Puppet agent.

To avoid the need to constantly pass the correct name of our master on the command line, add it to the [main] section in puppet.conf on the agent:

```
[main]
server=master.example.net
```

The agent's life cycle

In a Puppet-centric workflow, you typically want all changes to the configuration of servers (perhaps even workstations) to originate on the Puppet master and propagate to the agents automatically. Each new machine gets integrated into the Puppet infrastructure, with the master at its center, and gets removed during the decommissioning, as shown in the following diagram:

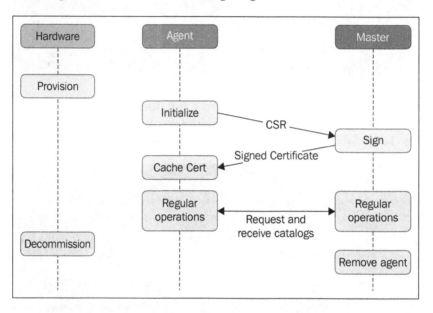

The very first step—generating a key and a certificate signing request—is always performed implicitly and automatically at the start of an agent run if no local SSL data exists yet. Puppet creates the required data if no appropriate files are found. There will be a short description on how to trigger this behavior manually later in this section.

The next step is usually the signing of the agent's certificate, which is performed on the master. It is a good practice to monitor the pending requests by listing them on the console:

```
root@puppetmaster# puppet cert list
root@puppetmaster# puppet cert sign '<agent fqdn>'
```

From this point on, the agent will periodically check with the master to load updated catalogs. The default interval for this is 30 minutes. The agent will perform a run of the catalog each time and check the sync state of all contained resources. The run is performed for unchanged catalogs as well, because the sync states can change between runs. Launching this background process can be done manually through a simple command:

```
root@agent# puppet agent
```

However, it is preferable to do this through the Puppet system service.

When an agent machine is taken out of active service, its certificate should be invalidated. As is customary with SSL, this is done through **revocation**. The master adds the serial number of the certificate to its certificate revocation list. This list, too, is shared with each agent machine. Revocation is initiated on the master through the `puppet cert` command:

```
root@puppetmaster# puppet cert --revoke agent
```

 The updated CRL is not honored until the master process is restarted. If security is a concern, this step must not be postponed.

The agent can then no longer use its old certificate:

```
root@agent# puppet agent --test
Warning: Unable to fetch my node definition, but the agent run wi
ll continue:
Warning: SSL_connect returned=1 errno=0 state=SSLv3 read server s
ession ticket A: sslv3 alert certificate revoked
```

Renewing an agent's certificate

Sometimes, it is necessary during an agent machine's life cycle to regenerate its certificate and related data—the reasons can include data loss, Human Error, or certificate expiration, among others. Performing the regeneration is quite simple: all relevant files are kept at /var/lib/puppet/ssl on the agent machine. Once these files are removed (or rather, the whole ssl/ directory tree), Puppet will renew everything on the next agent run. Of course, a new certificate must be signed. This requires some preparation—just initiating the request from the agent will fail.

```
root@agent# puppet agent --test
Info: Creating a new SSL key for agent
Info: Caching certificate for ca
Info: Caching certificate for agent
Error: Could not request certificate: The certificate retrieved f
rom the master does not match the agent's private key.
Certificate fingerprint: 95:D2:DD:31:AB:9C:FE:D7:A7:42:67:02:AE:3
A:7D:13:9E:D3:EF:06:9A:32:F5:88:E8:0D:80:9F:7D:FF:E9:FD
To fix this, remove the certificate from both the master and the
agent and then start a puppet run, which will automatically regen
erate a certficate.
On the master:
  puppet cert clean agent
On the agent:
  rm -f /var/lib/puppet/ssl/certs/agent.pem
  puppet agent -t
```

The master still has the old certificate cached. This is a simple protection against the impersonation of your agents by unauthorized entities. Once you perform the cleanup operation on the master, as advised in the preceding output, and remove the indicated file from the agent machine, the agent will be able to successfully place its new CSR:

```
root@puppet# puppet cert clean agent
Info: Caching certificate for agent
Notice: Revoked certificate with serial 18
Notice: Removing file Puppet::SSL::Certificate agent at '/var/lib/
puppet/ssl/ca/signed/agent.pem'
Notice: Removing file Puppet::SSL::Certificate agent at '/var/lib/
puppet/ssl/certs/agent.pem'
```

The rest of the process is identical to the original certificate creation. The agent uploads its CSR to the master, where the certificate is created through the puppet cert sign command.

Running the agent from cron

There is an alternative way to operate the agent. Instead of starting one long-running `puppet agent` process that does its work in set intervals and then goes back to sleep, it is also possible to have cron launch a discrete agent process in the same interval. This agent will contact the master once, run the received catalog, and then terminate. This has several advantages:

- The agent operating system saves some resources
- The interval is precise and not subject to skew (when running the background agent, deviations result from the time that elapses during the catalog run), and distributed interval skew can lead to thundering herd effects
- Any agent crashes or an inadvertent termination is not fatal

While crashes are becoming increasingly rare as the software matures, there is still an opportunity to cause the agent to stop unexpectedly. For example, some operating system packages have been known to restart the Puppet service during their update operation. However, if the Puppet agent itself was initiating the update (through a `package` resource), the restart of Puppet would cause the whole update to fail, because the post-installation script process killed one of its own ancestors (the agent process). Since the script failed right after stopping the agent, nothing would start it up again—manual intervention was necessary. Such scenarios can be avoided, but if the agent is run by cron, the risk is eliminated as a whole.

Setting Puppet to run the agent from cron is also very easy to do—with Puppet! You can use a manifest such as the following:

```
service {
    'puppet': enable => false
}
cron {
    'puppet-agent-run':
        user    => 'root',
        command =>
          'puppet agent --no-daemonize --onetime --logdest=syslog',
        minute  => fqdn_rand(60),
        hour    => absent,
}
```

The `fqdn_rand` function computes a distinct minute for each of your agents. Setting the `hour` property to `absent` means that the job should run every hour.

Performance considerations

Operating a Puppet master gives you numerous benefits over just using `puppet apply` on all your machines. This comes at a cost, of course. The master and agents form a server/client relation, and as with most such constructs, the server can become the bottleneck.

The good news is that the Puppet agent is a fat client. The major share of the work—inspecting file contents, interfacing with the package-management subsystem, services subsystem, and much more—is done by the agent. The master *"only"* has to compile manifests and build catalogs from them. This becomes increasingly complex as you hand over more control to Puppet.

There is one more task your master is responsible for. Many of your manifests will contain file resources that rely on prepared content:

```
file {
    '/usr/local/etc/my_app.ini':
        ensure => present,
        owner  => 'root',
        group  => 'root',
        source =>
            'puppet:///modules/my_app/usr/local/etc/my_app.ini',
}
```

The `source` parameter with a URL value indicates that the file has been pregenerated and placed in a module on the Puppet master (more on modules in *Chapter 5, Extending Your Puppet Infrastructure with Modules*). The agent will compare the local file with the master's copy (by checksum) and download the canonical version, if required. The comparison is a frequent occurrence in most agent runs—you will make Puppet manage lots of files. The master does not need lots of resources to make this happen, but it *will* hinder fluent agent operation if the master gets congested.

This can happen for any combination of these reasons:

- The total number of agents is too large
- The agents check-in too frequently
- The manifests are too complex
- The master's hardware resources are insufficient

There are ways to scale your master operation via load balancing, but these are not covered in this book.

Puppet Labs have some documentation on a few advanced approaches at `https://docs.puppetlabs.com/guides/scaling_multiple_masters.html`.

However, there is one essential optimization step in order to enable the master to use the hardware efficiently in the first place. This step will be detailed in the next section.

 Some advanced users have found it even more beneficial to remove the master from their Puppet infrastructure altogether. This approach can lead to elegant setups if done right, but an agent and master structure is easier to maintain, especially for new users.

Switching to Phusion Passenger

When launched via `puppet master` (or the system service), Puppet implements its HTTP interactions through the WEBrick library. This built-in server provides a reliable interface and little overhead for the application but really has no way of scaling, as Puppet is not multithreaded. As such, the WEBrick-based master is hardly fit for production and should usually be used for testing purposes only. For scalable low-latency operations, Puppet can rely on the industry standard for Ruby-based web applications—Passenger.

 The Puppet Labs documentation contains portable instructions for installing Passenger from the Ruby gem. Many users might prefer the stability of packages from the software-distribution maintainers. The following instructions rely on Debian packages.

Make sure that the standalone master process is stopped before setting up Apache with `mod_passenger`. This is not the only way to use Passenger, but it's one of the most popular ways:

1. You need to install the following package and its dependencies:

   ```
   root@puppetmaster# apt-get install libapache2-mod-passenger
   ```

2. Make sure the necessary Apache modules are active:

   ```
   root@puppetmaster# a2enmod ssl
   root@puppetmaster# a2enmod headers
   root@puppetmaster# a2enmod passenger
   ```

3. The Debian packages from Puppet Labs ship with example configurations you can use. Copy the virtual host definition to /etc/apache2 and enable it:

```
root@puppetmaster# cp /usr/share/puppet/ext/rack/example-passenger
-vhost.conf /etc/apache2/sites-available/puppetmaster
root@puppetmaster# a2ensite puppetmaster
```

4. Inside this configuration file, the SSL certificate name and location must be customized to match your setup:

```
SSLCertificateFile \
    /var/lib/puppet/ssl/certs/master.example.net.pem
SSLCertificateKeyFile \
    /var/lib/puppet/ssl/private_keys/master.example.net.pem
SSLCertificateChainFile /var/lib/puppet/ssl/ca/ca_crt.pem
SSLCACertificateFile    /var/lib/puppet/ssl/ca/ca_crt.pem
SSLCARevocationFile     /var/lib/puppet/ssl/ca/ca_crl.pem
```

The example virtual host defaults to locating the Puppet rack application at /etc/puppet/rack:

```
DocumentRoot /etc/puppet/rack/public
RackBaseURI /
<Directory /etc/puppet/rack/>
    . . .
```

5. You can customize the rack location, but let's just use this preset. Create the necessary directories, place the config.ru file there (again, copied from the Debian package), and make sure it has the correct ownership:

```
root@puppetmaster# mkdir -p /etc/puppet/rack/{tmp,public}
root@puppetmaster# install -o puppet -g puppet /usr/share/puppet/
rack/config.ru /etc/puppet/rack
```

6. Now everything is in place — restart the Apache service to make sure that the new port settings are applied:

```
root@puppetmaster# /etc/init.d/apache2 restart
```

From now on, your master service is available via Apache.

Using Passenger with Nginx

Nginx is a lean and fast web server that is ever increasing in popularity. It can run your Puppet master through Passenger as well, so you don't need to install Apache. Unfortunately, the stock version of Nginx cannot run Passenger through a module. The Phusion project supplies packages for the more popular Linux distributions, but only those that are for Debian and Ubuntu are current. On Red Hat derivatives, you will need to build Nginx yourself. Supporting packages that make this easy are available. The following instructions are applicable to Debian:

1. Follow the instructions at `https://www.phusionpassenger.com/documentation/Users%20guide%20Nginx.html#install_on_debian_ubuntu` in order to install appropriate Nginx packages.

2. In the `/etc/nginx/nginx.conf` file, uncomment or insert the `passenger` specific statements:

    ```
    passenger_root /usr/lib/ruby/vendor_ruby/phusion_passenger/
    locations.ini;
    passenger_ruby /usr/bin/ruby;
    ```

3. Prepare the `Rails` configuration just like you would for Apache:

    ```
    root@puppetmaster# mkdir -p /etc/puppet/rack/{tmp,public}

    root@puppetmaster# install -o puppet -g puppet /usr/share/puppet/
    rack/config.ru /etc/puppet/rack
    ```

4. Create a vhost for Puppet at `/etc/nginx/sites-available/puppetmaster`:

    ```
    server {
            listen 8140;
            server_name master.example.net;
            root /etc/puppet/rack/public;

            ssl on;
            ssl_certificate
                    /var/lib/puppet/ssl/certs/master.example.net.pem;
            ssl_certificate_key
              /var/lib/puppet/ssl/private_keys/master.example.net.pem;
            ssl_crl /var/lib/puppet/ssl/ca/ca_crl.pem;
            ssl_client_certificate   /var/lib/puppet/ssl/certs/ca.pem;
            ssl_verify_client optional;
            ssl_verify_depth 1;

            passenger_enabled on;
            passenger_set_cgi_param HTTPS on;
    ```

```
                    passenger_set_cgi_param SSL_CLIENT_S_DN $ssl_client_s_dn;
                    passenger_set_cgi_param
                        SSL_CLIENT_VERIFY $ssl_client_verify;
        }
```

5. Enable the vhost and restart Nginx:

    ```
    root@puppetmaster# ln -s ../sites-available/puppetmaster/ etc/
    nginx/sites-enabled/puppetmaster

    root@puppetmaster# /etc/init.d/nginx restart
    ```

Nginx is now running the Puppet master service for you through Passenger. The mentioned configuration is bareboned, and you might wish to extend it for tuning and features. The next section is written with Apache in mind, but the concepts can be applied to Nginx just as well.

Basic tuning

There is really only one important value that you should scale to your circumstances — the Passenger pool size. It determines how many Ruby processes Apache is allowed to fork and run in parallel.

Again, Puppet is inherently single-threaded. Each incoming request is handed to a `puppet master` process, which then single-mindedly goes about its business. Compiling manifests is usually limited by the CPU power — until finished, the master process will use one processor core fully. Assuming that there is no shortage of memory and I/O operations, you can optimize the throughput of the master by sizing the Passenger pool to a number equal to or just below your number of available processor cores. Allowing too many parallel processes can lead to CPU congestion and degraded total performance due to the context-switching overhead. An undersized pool might waste CPU resources.

> The Puppet toolchain can help you determine the exact
> number of CPU cores available to your operating system.
> Try running `facter processorcount`. The next chapter
> contains more information on this topic.

If the frequency of catalog requests substantially exceeds the maximum throughput of your pool, you will notice issues. Catalog requests might fail because no worker accepts them in time. During catalog runs, file resources can fail because no master can be reached to supply the checksum. If you cannot upgrade your master, you can trade some performance for stability instead. Do this by enlarging the pool beyond the number of processors, after all.

For the small virtual machine used for all examples in this book, I limited Passenger to two parallel master processes:

```
PassengerHighPerformance on
PassengerPoolSize 2
...
```

The tuning settings are predefined in the sample virtual host configuration as well.

Troubleshooting SSL issues

Among the most frustrating issues, especially for new users, are problems with the agent's SSL handshake. Such errors are especially troublesome because Puppet cannot always offer very helpful analysis in its logs—the problems occur in the SSL library functions, and the application cannot examine the circumstances.

The online documentation at Puppet Labs has a **Troubleshooting** section that has some advice concerning SSL-related issues as well at https://docs.puppetlabs.com/guides/troubleshooting.html.

SSL errors are reported by the agent just like other failures:

```
root@agent# puppet agent --test
Warning: Unable to fetch my node definition, but the agent run wi
ll continue:
Warning: SSL_connect returned=1 errno=0 state=SSLv3 read server c
ertificate B: certificate verify failed: [CRL is not yet valid fo
r /CN=master.example.net]
```

The agent opines that the CRL it receives from the master is not yet valid. Errors like these can happen whenever the agent's clock gets reset to a very early date. This can also result from but a slight clock skew, when the CRL has very recently been updated through a revocation action on the master. If the system clock on the agent machine returns a time far in the future, it will consider certificates to be expired.

These clock-related issues are best avoided by running an ntp service on all Puppet agents and masters.

Errors will generally result if the data in the agent's `/var/lib/puppet/ssl` tree becomes inconsistent. This can happen when the agent interacts with an alternate master (a testing instance, for example). The first piece of advice you will most likely receive when asking the community what to do about such problems is to create a new agent certificate from scratch. This works as described in the *The agent's life cycle* section:

1. Remove all the SSL data from the agent machine.
2. Revoke and remove the certificate from the master using `puppet cert clean`.
3. Request and sign a new certificate.

This approach will indeed remedy most issues. Be careful not to leave any old files in the relevant location on the agent machine. If the problems persist, a more involved solution is required. The `openssl` command-line tool is helpful for analyzing the certificates and related files. The details of such an analysis are beyond the scope of this book, though.

Summary

You can now set up your own Puppet master, either in a simple testing setup using WEBrick or a more scalable setup with Passenger. There was also a short discussion on tuning Apache for your needs. You have successfully signed the certificate for a Puppet agent and can revoke certificates, if required. Using the `node` blocks in the master manifest, you can describe individual manifests for each distinct agent. Finally, you learned about some things that can go wrong with the SSL-based authentication.

In the next chapter, we will take a look at the inner workings of Puppet in order to give you an understanding of how the Puppet agent adapts itself to its environment. You will also learn how the agent provides feedback to the master, allowing you to create flexible manifests that fit different needs.

3
A Peek Under the Hood – Facts, Types, and Providers

So far in this book, you have primarily done practical things—writing manifests, setting up a master, agents, Passenger, and so forth. Before you are introduced to the missing language concepts that you will need to use Puppet effectively for bigger projects, there is some background that we should cover first. Don't worry, it won't be all dry theory—most of the important parts of Puppet are relevant to your daily business.

The topics for this chapter have been hinted at earlier; *Chapter 1*, *Writing Your First Manifests*, contained a brief description of the type and provider subsystem, and *Chapter 2*, *The Master and Its Agents*, mentioned Facter as a means to get some information about your master hardware. These elementary topics will be thoroughly explored in the following sections:

- Summarizing systems with Facter
- Understanding the type system
- Substantiating the model with providers
- Putting it all together

Summarizing systems with Facter

Configuration management is quite a dynamic problem. In other words, the systems that need configuration are mostly moving targets. In some situations, system administrators or operators get lucky and work with large quantities of 100 percent uniform hardware and software. In most cases, however, the landscape of servers and other computing nodes is rather heterogeneous, at least in subtle ways. Even in unified networks, there are likely multiple generations of machines, with small or larger differences required for their respective configurations.

For example, a common task for Puppet is to handle the configuration of system monitoring. Your business logic will likely dictate warning thresholds for gauges such as the system load value. However, those thresholds can rarely be static. On a two-processor virtual machine, a system load of 10 represents a crippling overload, while the same value can be absolutely acceptable for a busy DBMS server that has cutting-edge hardware of the largest dimensions.

Another important factor can be software platforms. Your infrastructure might span multiple distributions of Linux, or alternate operating systems such as BSD, Solaris, or Windows, each with different ways of handling certain scenarios. Imagine, for example, that you want Puppet to manage some content of the fstab file. On your rare Solaris system, you would have to make sure that Puppet targets the /etc/vfstab file instead of /etc/fstab.

It is usually not a good idea to interact with the fstab file in your manifest directly. This example will be rounded off in the section concerning providers.

Puppet strives to present you with a unified way of managing all of your infrastructure. It obviously needs a means to allow your manifests to adapt to different kinds of circumstances on the agent machines. This includes their operating system, hardware layout, and many other details. Keep in mind that generally, the manifests have to be compiled on the master machine.

There are several conceivable ways to implement a solution for this particular problem. A direct approach would be a language construct that allows the master to send a piece of shell script (or other code) to the agent and receive its output in return.

The following is pseudocode however; there are no backtick expressions in the Puppet DSL:

```
if `grep -c ^processor /proc/cpuinfo` > 2 {
    $load_warning = 4
}
else {
    $load_warning = 2
}
```

This solution would be powerful but expensive. The master would need to call back to the agent whenever the compilation process encounters such an expression. Writing manifests that were able to cope if such a command had returned an error code would be strenuous, and Puppet would likely end up resembling a quirky scripting engine.

When using `puppet apply` instead of the master, such a feature would pose less of a problem, and it is indeed available in the form of the `generate` function, which works just like the backticks in the pseudocode mentioned previously. The commands are always run on the compiling node though, so this is less useful with an agent/master than `apply`.

Puppet uses a different approach. It relies on a secondary system called Facter, which has the sole purpose of examining the machine on which it is run. It serves a list of well-known variable names and values, all according to the system on which it runs. For example, an actual Puppet manifest that needs to form a condition upon the number of processors on the agent will use this expression:

```
if $processorcount > 4 { … }
```

Facter's variables are called **facts**, and `processorcount` is such a fact. The fact values are gathered by the agent just before it requests its catalog from the master. All fact names and values are transferred to the master as part of the request. They are available in the manifest as variables.

Facts are available to manifests that are used with `puppet apply` too, of course. You can test this very simply:

```
puppet apply -e 'notify { "I am $fqdn and have
$processorcount CPUs": }'
```

Accessing and using fact values

You have already seen an example use of the `processorcount` fact. In the manifest, each fact value is available as a global variable value. That is why you can just use the `$processorcount` expression where you need it.

> You will often see conventional uses such as `$::processorcount` or `$::ipaddress`. Prefixing the fact name with double colons was a good idea in older Puppet versions before 3.0. The official *Style Guide* at `https://docs.puppetlabs.com/guides/style_guide.html#namespacing-variables` is outdated in this regard and still recommends this. The prefix is no longer necessary.

Some helpful facts have already been mentioned. The `processorcount` fact might play a role for your configuration. When configuring some services, you will want to use the machine's `ipaddress` value in a configuration file or as an argument value:

```
file {
    '/etc/mysql/conf.d/bind-address':
        ensure  => 'file',
        mode    => '644',
        content => "[mysqld]\nbind-address=$ipaddress\n",
}
```

Besides the hostname, your manifest can also make use of the **fully qualified domain name (FQDN)** of the agent machine.

> The agent will use the value of its `fqdn` fact as the name of its certificate (`clientcert`) by default. The master receives both these values. Note that the agent can override the `fqdn` value to any name, whereas the `clientcert` value is tied to the signed certificate that the agent uses. Sometimes, you will want the master to pass sensitive information to individual nodes. The manifest must identify the agent by its `clientcert` fact and never use `fqdn` or `hostname` instead, for the reason mentioned. An example is shown in the following code:
>
> ```
> file {
>     '/etc/my-secret':
>         ensure => 'file',
>         mode   => '600',
>         owner  => 'root',
>         source =>
>             "puppet:///modules/secrets/$clientcert/key",
> }
> ```

There is a whole group of facts to describe the operating system. Each fact is useful in different situations. The operatingsystem fact takes values such as Debian or CentOS:

```
if $operatingsystem != 'Ubuntu' {
    package {
        'avahi-daemon':
            ensure => absent
    }
}
```

If your manifest will behave identical for RHEL, CentOS, and Fedora (but not on Debian and Ubuntu), you will make use of the osfamily fact instead:

```
if $osfamily == 'RedHat' {
    $kernel_package = 'kernel'
}
```

The operatingsystemrelease fact allows you to tailor your manifests to differences between the versions of your OS:

```
if $operatingsystem == 'Debian' {
    if versioncmp($operatingsystemrelease, '7.0') >= 0 {
        $ssh_ecdsa_support = true
    }
}
```

Facts such as macaddress, the different SSH host keys, fingerprints, and others make it easy to use Puppet for keeping inventory of your hardware. There is a slew of other useful facts. Of course, the collection will not suit every possible need of every user out there. That is why Facter comes readily extendible.

Extending Facter with custom facts

Technically, nothing is stopping you from adding your own fact code right next to the core facts, either by maintaining your own Facter package, or even deploying the Ruby code files to your agents directly through Puppet management. However, Puppet offers a much more convenient alternative in the form of **custom facts**.

We have still not covered Puppet modules yet. They will be thoroughly introduced in *Chapter 5*, *Extending Your Puppet Infrastructure with Modules*. For now, just create a Ruby file at /etc/puppet/modules/hello_world/lib/facter/hello.rb on the master machine. Puppet will recognize this as a custom fact of the name hello.

The inner workings of Facter are very straightforward and goal oriented. There is one block of Ruby code for each fact, and the return value of the block becomes the fact value. Many facts are self-sufficient, but others will rely on the values of one or more basic facts. For example, the method for determining the IP address(es) of the local machine is highly dependent upon the operating system.

The `hello` fact is very simple though:

```
Facter.add(:hello) do
  setcode { "Hello, world!" }
end
```

The return value of the `setcode` block is the string, `Hello, world!`, and you can use this fact as `$hello` in a Puppet manifest.

> Before Facter Version 2.0, each fact had a string value. If a code block returns another value, such as an array or hash, Facter 1.x will convert it to a string. The result is not useful in many cases. For this historic reason, there are facts such as `ipaddress_eth0` and `ipaddress_lo`, instead of (or in addition to) a proper hash structure with interface names and addresses.

It is important for the `pluginsync` option to be enabled on the agent side. This has been the default for a long time and should not require any customization. The agent will synchronize all custom facts whenever checking in to the master. They are permanently available on the agent machine after that. You can then retrieve the `hello` fact from the command line using `facter -p hello`. By just invoking `facter` without an argument, you request a list of all fact names and values.

> When testing your custom facts from the command line, you need to invoke `facter` with the `-p` or `--puppet` option. Puppet itself will *always* include the custom facts.

This book will not cover all aspects of Facter's API, but there is one facility that is quite essential. Many of your custom facts will only be useful on Unix-like systems, and others will only be useful on your Windows boxen. You can retrieve such values using a construct like the following:

```
if Facter.value(:kernel) != "windows"
  nil
else
  # actual fact code here
end
```

This would be quite tedious and repetitive though. Instead, you can invoke the `confine` method within the `Facter.add(name) { ... }` block:

```
Facter.add(:msvs_version) do
  confine :kernel => :windows
  setcode do
    # ...
  end
end
```

You can confine a fact to several alternative values as well:

```
confine :kernel => [ :linux, :sunos ]
```

Finally, if a fact does make sense in different circumstances, but requires drastically different code in each respective case, you can add the same fact several times, each with a different set of `confine` values. Core facts such as `ipaddress` use this often:

```
Facter.add(:ipaddress) do
  confine :kernel => :linux
  ...
end
Facter.add(:ipaddress) do
  confine :kernel => %w{FreeBSD OpenBSD Darwin DragonFly}
  ...
end
...
```

You can confine facts based on any combination of other facts, not just `kernel`. It is a very popular choice, though. The `operatingsystem` or `osfamily` fact can be more appropriate in certain situations. Technically, you can even confine some of your facts to certain `processorcount` values and so forth.

Simplifying things using external facts

If writing and maintaining Ruby code is not desirable in your team for any reason, you might prefer to use an alternative that allows shell scripts, or really any kind of programming language, or even static data with no programming involved at all. Facter allows this in the form of **external facts**.

Creating an external fact is similar to the process for regular custom facts, with the following distinctions:

- Facts are produced by standalone executables or files with static data, which the agent must find in `/etc/facter/facts.d`

- The data is not just a string value, but an arbitrary number of `key=value` pairs instead

The data need not use the `ini` file notation style—the key/value pairs can also be in the YAML or JSON format. The following external facts hold the same data:

```
# site-facts.txt
workgroup=CT4Site2
domain_psk=nm56DxLp%
```

The facts can be written in the YAML format in the following way:

```
# site-facts.yaml
workgroup: CT4Site2
domain_psk: nm56DxLp%
```

In the JSON format, facts can be written as follows:

```
# site-facts.json
{ 'workgroup': 'CT4Site2', 'domain_psk': 'nm56DxLp%' }
```

The deployment of the external facts works simply through `file` resources in your Puppet manifest:

```
file {
    '/etc/facter/facts.d/site-facts.yaml':
        ensure => 'file',
        source => 'puppet:///…',
}
```

 With newer versions of Puppet and Facter, external facts will be automatically synchronized just like custom facts if they are found in `facts.d/*` in any module (for example, `/etc/puppet/modules/hello_world/facts.d/hello.sh`). This is not only more convenient, but has a large benefit: when Puppet must fetch an external fact through a `file` resource instead, its fact value(s) are not yet available while the catalog is being compiled. The `pluginsync` mechanism, on the other hand, makes sure that all synced facts are available before manifest compilation starts.

When facts are not static and cannot be placed in a `txt` or YAML file, you can make the file executable instead. It will usually be a shell script, but the implementation is of no consequence; it is just important that properly formatted data is written to the standard output. You can simplify the `hello` fact this way, in `/etc/puppet/modules/hello_world/facts.d/hello`:

```
#!/bin/sh

echo hello=Hello, world\!
```

For executable facts, the `ini` styled `key=value` format is the only supported one. YAML or JSON are not eligible in this context.

Goals of Facter

The whole structure and philosophy of Facter serves the goal of allowing for platform-agnostic usage and development. The same collection of facts (roughly) is available on all supported platforms. This allows Puppet users to keep a coherent development style through manifests for all those different systems.

Facter forms a layer of abstraction over the characteristics of both hardware and software. It is an important piece of Puppet's platform-independent architecture. Another piece that was mentioned before is the type and provider subsystem. Types and providers are explored in greater detail in the following sections.

Understanding the type system

Being one of the cornerstones of the Puppet model, resources were introduced quite early in *Chapter 1, Writing Your First Manifests*. Remember how each resource represents a piece of state on the agent system. It has a resource type, a name (or a title), and a list of attributes. An attribute can either be `property` or `parameter`. Between the two of them, properties represent distinct pieces of state, and parameters merely influence Puppet's actions upon the `property` values.

Let's examine resource types in more detail and understand their inner workings. This is not only important when extending Puppet with resource types of your own (which will be demonstrated in *Chapter 5, Extending Your Puppet Infrastructure with Modules*). It also helps you anticipate the action that Puppet will take, given your manifest, and get a better understanding of both the master and the agent.

First, we take a closer look at the operational structure of Puppet, with its pieces and phases. The agent performs all its work in discreet **transactions**. A transaction is started under any of the following circumstances:

- The background agent process activates and checks in to the master
- An agent process is started with the `--onetime` or `--test` option
- A local manifest is compiled using `puppet apply`

The transaction always passes several stages:

1. Gathering fact values to form the actual catalog request.
2. Receiving the compiled catalog from the master.

3. Prefetching of current resource states.

4. Validation of the catalog's content.

5. Synchronization of the system with the `property` values from the catalog.

Facter was explained in the previous section. The resource types become important during compilation and then throughout the rest of the agent transaction. The master loads all resource types to perform some basic checking—it basically makes sure that the types of resources it finds in the manifests do exist and that the attribute names fit the respective type.

The resource type's life cycle on the agent side

Once the compilation has succeeded, the master hands out the catalog and the agent enters the catalog validation phase. Each resource type can define some Ruby methods that ensure that the passed values make sense. This happens on two levels of granularity: each attribute can validate its input value, and then the resource as a whole can be checked for consistency.

One example for attribute value validation can be found in the `ssh_authorized_key` resource type. A resource of this type fails if its `key` value contains a whitespace character, because SSH keys cannot comprise multiple strings.

Validation of whole resources happens with the `cron` type for example. It makes sure that the `time` fields make sense together. The following resource would not pass, because special times such as `@midgnight` cannot be combined with numeric fields:

```
cron {
    'invalid-resource':
        command => 'rm -rf /',
        special => 'midnight',
        weekday => [ '2', '5' ],
}
```

Another task during this phase is the transformation of input values to more suitable internal representations. The resource type code refers to this as a `munge` action. Typical examples of munging are the removal of leading and trailing whitespace from string values, or the conversion of array values to an appropriate string format—this can be a comma-separated list, but for search paths, the separator should be a colon instead. Other kinds of values will use different representations.

Next up is the prefetching phase. Some resource types allow the agent to create an internal list of resource instances that are present on the system. For example, this is possible (and makes sense) for installed packages—Puppet can just invoke the package manager to produce the list. For other types, such as `file`, this would not be prudent. Creating a list of all reachable paths in the whole filesystem can be arbitrarily expensive, depending on the system on which the agent is running.

Finally, the agent starts walking its internal graph of interdependent resources. Each resource is brought in sync if necessary. This happens separately for each individual property, for the most part.

 The `ensure` property, for types that support it, is a notable exception. It is expected to manage all other properties on its own—when a resource is changed from `absent` to `present` through its `ensure` property (in other words, the resource is getting newly created), this action should bring all other properties in sync as well.

There are some notable aspects of the whole agent process. For one, attributes are handled independently. Each can define its own methods for the different phases. There are quite a number of hooks, which allow a resource type author to add a lot of flexibility to the model.

 For aspiring type authors, skimming through the core types can be quite inspirational. You will be familiar with many attributes, through using them in your manifests and studying their hooks will offer quite some insight.

It is also worth noting that the whole validation process is performed by the agent, not the master. This is beneficial in terms of performance. The master saves a lot of work, which gets distributed to the network of agents (which scales with your needs automatically).

Substantiating the model with providers

At the start of this chapter, you learned about Facter and how it works like a layer of abstraction over the supported platforms. This unified information base is one of Puppet's most important means to achieve its goal of operating system independence. Another one is the DSL, of course. Finally, Puppet also needs a method to transparently adapt its behavior to the respective platform on which each agent runs.

In other words, depending on the characteristics of the computing environment, the agent needs to switch between different implementations for its resources. This is not unlike object-oriented programming – the type system provides a unified interface, like an abstract base class. The programmer need not worry what specific class is being referenced, as long as it correctly implements all required methods. In this analogy, Puppet's providers are the concrete classes that implement the abstract interface.

For a practical example, look at package management. Different flavors of UNIX-like operating systems have their own implementation. The most prevalent Puppet platforms use `apt` and `yum`, respectively, but can (and sometimes must) also manage their packages through `dpkg` and `rpm`. Other platforms use tools such as `emerge`, `zypper`, `fink`, and a slew of other things. There are even packages that exist apart from the operating system software base, handled through `gem`, `pip`, and other language-specific package management tools. For each of these management tools, there is a provider for the package type.

Many of these tools allow the same set of operations – install and uninstall a package and update a package to a specific version. The latter is not universally possible though. For example, `dpkg` can only ever install the local package that is specified on the command line, with no other version to choose. There are also some distinct features that are unique to specific tools, or supported by only a few. Some management systems can hold packages at specific versions. Some use different states for uninstalled versus purged packages. Some have a notion of virtual packages. There are some more examples.

Because of this potential diversity (which is not limited to package management systems), Puppet providers can opt for **features**. The set of features is resource type specific. All providers for a type can support one or more of the same group of features. For the `package` type, there are features such as `versionable`, `purgeable`, `holdable`, and so forth. You can set `ensure => purged` on any package resource like so:

```
package {
    'haproxy':
        ensure => 'purged'
}
```

However, if you are managing the `HAproxy` package through `rpm`, Puppet will fail to make any sense of that, because `rpm` has no notion of a `purged` state, and therefore the `purgeable` feature is missing from the `rpm` provider. Trying to use an unsupported feature will usually produce an error message. Some attributes (such as `install_options`) might just get ignored by Puppet instead.

The official documentation on the Puppet Labs website holds a complete list of the core resource types and all their built-in providers, along with the respective feature matrices. It is very easy to find suitable providers and their capabilities; the documentation is at `https://docs.puppetlabs.com/references/latest/type.html`.

Providerless resource types

There are some resource types that use no providers, but they are rare among the core types. Most of the interesting management tasks that Puppet makes easy just work differently among operating systems, and providers enable this in a most elegant fashion.

Even for straightforward tasks that are the same on all platforms, there might be a provider. For example, there is a `host` type to manage entries in the `/etc/hosts` file. Its syntax is universal, so the code can technically just be implemented in the type. However, there are actual abstract base classes for certain kinds of providers in the Puppet code base. One of them makes it very easy to build providers that edit files if those files consist of single-line records with ordered fields. Therefore, it makes sense to implement a provider for the `host` type and base it on this provider class.

For the curious, this is what a `host` resource looks like:

```
host { 'puppet':
    ip => '10.144.12.100',
    host_aliases => [ 'puppet.example.net', 'master' ]
}
```

Summarizing types and providers

Puppet's resource types and their providers work together to form a solid abstraction layer over software configuration details. The type system is an extendable basis for Puppet's powerful DSL. It forms an elaborate interface for the polymorphous provider layer.

The providers flexibly implement the actual management actions that Puppet is supposed to perform. They map the necessary synchronization steps to commands and system interactions. Many providers cannot satisfy every nuance that the resource type models. The feature system takes care of these disparities in a transparent fashion.

Putting it all together

Reading this far, you might have gotten the impression that this chapter is a rather odd mix of topics. While types and providers do belong closely together, the whole introduction to Facter might seem out of place in their context. This is deceptive however: facts do play a vital part in the type/provider structure. They are essential for Puppet to make good choices among providers.

Let's look at an example from the *Extending Facter with custom facts* section once more. It was about `fstab` entries and the difference of Solaris, where those are found in `/etc/vfstab` instead of `/etc/fstab`. That section suggested a manifest that adapts according to a fact value. As you can imagine now, Puppet has a resource type to manage `fstab` content: the `mount` type. However, for the small deviation of a different file path, there is no dedicated `mount` provider for Solaris. There is actually just one provider for all platforms, but on Solaris, it behaves differently. It does this by resolving Facter's `osfamily` value. The following code example was adapted from the actual provider code:

```
case Facter.value(:osfamily)
when "Solaris"
  fstab = "/etc/vfstab"
else
  fstab = "/etc/fstab"
end
```

In other cases, Puppet should use thoroughly different providers on different platforms, though. Package management is a classic example. On a Red Hat-like platform, you will want Puppet to use the `yum` provider in virtually all cases. It can be sensible to use `rpm`, and even `apt` might be available. However, if you tell Puppet to make sure a package is installed, you expect it to install it using `yum` if necessary.

This is obviously a common theme. Certain management tasks need to be performed in different environments, with very different toolchains. In such cases, it is quite clear which provider would be best suited. To make this happen, a provider can declare itself the default if a condition is met. In the case of `yum`, it is the following:

```
defaultfor :operatingsystem => [:fedora, :centos, :redhat]
```

The conditions are based around fact values. If the `operatingsystem` value for a given agent is among the listed, `yum` will consider itself the default package provider.

> The `operatingsystem` and `osfamily` facts are the most popular choices for such queries in providers, but any fact is eligible.

In addition to marking themselves as being default, there is more filtering of providers that relies on fact values. Providers can also confine themselves to certain combinations of values. For example, the `yum` alternative, `zypper`, confines itself to SUSE Linux distributions:

```
confine :operatingsystem => [:suse, :sles, :sled, :opensuse]
```

This provider method works just like the `confine` method in Facter, which was discussed earlier in this chapter. The provider will not even be seen as valid if the respective facts on the agent machine have none of the white-listed values.

> If you find yourself looking through code for some core providers, you will notice confinement (and even declaring default providers) on `feature` values, although there is no Facter fact of that name. These features are not related to provider features either. They are from another layer of introspection similar to Facter, but hardcoded into the Puppet agent. These agent features are a number of flags that identify some system properties that need not be made available to manifests in the form of facts. For example, the `posix` provider for the `exec` type becomes the default in the presence of the corresponding feature:
>
> ```
> defaultfor :feature => :posix
> ```

You will find that some providers forgo the `confine` method altogether, as it is not mandatory for correct agent operation. Puppet will also identify unsuitable providers when looking for their necessary operating system commands. For example, the `pw` provider for certain BSD flavors does not bother with a `confine` statement. It only declares its one required command:

```
commands :pw => "pw"
```

Agents that find no `pw` binary in their search path will not try and use this provider at all.

This concludes the little tour of the inner workings of types and providers with the help of Facter. For a complete example of building a provider for a type and using the internal tools that you have now learned about, you can refer to *Chapter 5, Extending Your Puppet Infrastructure with Modules*.

Summary

Puppet gathers information about all agent systems using Facter. The information base consists of a large number of independent bits, called facts. Manifests can query the values of those facts to adapt to the respective agents that trigger their compilation. Puppet also uses facts to choose among providers, the work horses that make the abstract resource types functional across the wide range of supported platforms.

The resource types not only completely define the interface that Puppet exposes in the DSL, they also take care of all validation of input values, transformations that must be performed before handing values to the providers and other related tasks.

The providers encapsulate all knowledge of actual operating systems and their respective toolchains. They implement the functionality that the resource types describe. The Puppet model's configurations apply to platforms, which vary from one another, so not every facet of every resource type can make sense for all agents. By exposing only the supported features, a provider can express such limitations.

After this in-depth look at the internal details, let's tackle more practical concerns again. The following chapters will cover the tools needed to build complex and advanced manifests of all scales.

Modularizing Manifests with Classes and Defined Types

At this point, you have already performed some production-grade tasks with Puppet. You learned how to write standalone manifests and then invoke `puppet apply` to put them to use. While setting up your first Puppet master and agent, you created a simple example for a node manifest on the master. In a `node 'hostname'` block, you created the equivalent of a manifest file. This way, the Puppet master used just this manifest for the specified agent node.

While this is all useful and of essential importance, it will obviously not suffice for daily business. By working with `node` blocks that contain sets of resources, you will end up performing lots of copy and paste operations for similar nodes, and the whole construct will become unwieldy very quickly.

This is an unnatural approach to developing Puppet manifests. Despite the great differences to many other languages that you might be familiar with, the Puppet DSL is a programming language. Building manifests merely from `node` blocks and resources would be like writing C with no functions except `main`, or Ruby without any classes of your own.

The manifests that you can write with the means that are already at your disposal are not flat—you learned about common control structures such as `if` and `case`. Your manifests can use these to adapt to various circumstances on the agent, by querying the values of Facter facts and branching in accordance to the results.

However, these constructs should be complemented by the language tools to create reusable units of manifest code, similar to functions or methods in procedural languages. This chapter introduces these concepts through the following topics:

- Introducing classes and defined types
- Structured design patterns
- Including classes from defined types
- Nesting definitions in classes
- Establishing relationships among containers
- Making classes more flexible through parameters

Introducing classes and defined types

Puppet's equivalent to methods or functions are twofold—there are **classes** on one hand and **defined types** (also just referred to as **defines**) on the other.

 You will find that the function analogy is a bit weak for classes, but fits defined types quite well.

Both are similar at first glance, in the way that they hold a chunk of reusable manifest code. There are big differences in the way each is used though. Let's take a look at classes first.

Defining and declaring classes

A Puppet class can be considered to be a container for resources. It is defined once and selected by all nodes that need to make use of the prepared functionality. Each class represents a well-known subset of a system's configuration.

For example, a classic use case is a class that installs the Apache web server and applies some basic settings. This class will look like the following:

```
class apache {
    package {
        'apache2':
            ensure => 'installed',
    }
    file {
        '/etc/apache2/apache2.conf':
            ensure  => 'file',
```

```
        source  =>
          'puppet:///modules/apache/etc/apache2/apache2.conf',
        require => Package['apache2'],
    }
    service {
        'apache2':
            enable  => true,
            require => Package['apache2'],
    }
}
```

All web server nodes will make use of this class. To this end, their manifests need to contain a simple statement:

```
include apache
```

This is referred to as **including** a class, or **declaring** it. If your apache class is powerful enough to do all that is needed, this line might fully comprise a node block's content:

```
node 'webserver01' {
    include apache
}
```

> In your own setup, you will likely not write your own Apache class. You can use open source classes that are available through **Puppet modules**. *Chapter 5, Extending Your Puppet Infrastructure with Modules*, will give you all the details.

This already concludes our tour of classes in a nutshell. There is yet some more to discuss, of course, but let's look at defined types before that.

Creating and using defined types

A defined type can be imagined like a blueprint for a piece of manifest. Like a class, it mainly consists of a body of the manifest code. However, a defined type takes arguments and makes their values available in its body as local variables.

Here is another typical example for a defined type, the Apache virtual host configuration:

```
define virtual_host($content,
                    $priority = '050') {
    file {
```

```
            "/etc/apache2/sites-available/$name":
                ensure  => 'file',
                owner   => 'root',
                group   => 'root',
                mode    => '644',
                content => $content;
            "/etc/apache2/sites-enabled/$priority-$name":
                ensure  => 'link',
                target  => "../sites-available/$name";
        }
    }
```

This code might still seem pretty cryptic. It should get clearer in the context of how it is actually used from other places in your manifest; the following code shows you how:

```
virtual_host {
    'example.net':
        content  =>  file('/etc/puppet/modules/apache2/files/vhosts/
                          example.net');
    'fallback':
        priority => '999',
        content  => file('/etc/puppet/modules/apache2/files/vhosts/
                          fallback');
}
```

This is why the construct is called a defined type—you can now place what appears to be resources in your manifest, but you really call your own manifest code construct.

> The official *Style Guide* forbids declaring multiple resources in one block, separated by a semicolon. It can be sensible to declare each resource in its own block, if they are unrelated:
>
> ```
> virtual_host {
>     'example.net':
>         content => ...,
> }
> virtual_host {
>     'example.net':
>         priority => '999',
>         content  => ...,
> }
> ```
>
> This is not always necessary and can even hurt readability. Whether you abide by the guide is up to your own discretion.

The `virtual_host` type takes two arguments: the `content` argument is mandatory and is used verbatim in the configuration file resource. Puppet will synchronize that file's content to what is specified in the manifest. The `priority` argument is optional. If omitted, the respective virtual host definition uses the default priority of `050` as the prefix.

Also, each defined type can implicitly refer to the name (or title) by which it was called. In other words, each instance of your define gets a name, and you can access it through the `$name` or `$title` variable.

There are a few other *magic* variables that are available in the body of a defined type. If a resource of the defined type is declared with a metaparameter such as `require => ...`, its value can be accessed through the `$require` variable in the body. The variable value is empty if the metaparameter is not used. This works for all metaparameters such as `before`, `notify`, and all others, but you will likely never need to make use of this. The metaparameters automatically do the right thing.

Understanding and leveraging the differences

The respective purposes of Puppet's class and defined type are very specific and they usually don't overlap.

The class declares resources and properties that are in some way centric to the system. A class is a finalized description of one or sometimes more aspects of your system as a whole. Whatever the class represents, it can only ever exist in one form; to Puppet, each class is implicitly a singleton, a fixed set of information that either applies to your system (the class is included) or not.

Typical resources you will encapsulate in a class for convenient inclusion in a manifest are as follows:

- One or more packages that should be installed (or removed)
- A specific configuration file in `/etc`
- A common directory, needed to store scripts or configs for many subsystems
- Cron jobs that should be mostly identical on all applicable systems

The define is used for all things that exist in multiple instances. All aspects that appear in varying quantities in your system can possibly be modeled using this language construct. In this regard, the define is very similar to the full-fledged resource it mimics with its declaration syntax. Some of the typical contents of defined types are:

- Files in a `conf.d` style directory
- Entries in an easily parseable file such as `/etc/hosts`
- Rules in a firewall

The class' singleton nature is especially valuable in that clashes in the form of multiple resource declarations are being prevented. Remember that each resource must be unique to a catalog. For example, consider another declaration:

```
package { 'apache2': }
```

This declaration can be anywhere in the manifest of one of your web servers (say, right in the `node` block next to `include apache`); this additional declaration will prevent the successful compilation of a catalog.

> The reason for the prevention of a successful compilation is that Puppet currently cannot make sure that both declarations represent the same target state, or can be merged to form a composite state. It is likely that multiple declarations of the same resource get in a conflict about the desired value of some property (for example, one declaration might want to ensure a package is `absent`, while the other needs it to be `present`).

The virtue of the class is that there can be an arbitrary number of `include` statements for the same class strewn throughout the manifest. Puppet will commit the class's contents to the catalog exactly once.

> Note that the uniqueness constraint for resources includes defined types. No two instances of your own define can share the same name. Using a name twice or more produces a compiler error:
>
> ```
> apache_vhost {
>     'wordpress':
>         content  => file(...),
>         priority => '011';
>     'wordpress':
>         content  => '# Dummy vhost',
>         priority => '600';
> }
> ```

Structured design patterns

Your knowledge of classes and defined types is still rather academic. You have learned about their defining aspects and the syntax to use them, but we have yet to give you a feeling of how these concepts come to bear in different real-life scenarios.

The following sections will present an overview of what you can do with these new language tools.

Writing comprehensive classes

Many classes are written to make Puppet perform momentous tasks on the agent platform. Of these, the Apache class is probably one of the more modest examples. You can conceive a class that can be included from any machine's manifest and make sure that:

- Firewalling software is installed and configured with a default ruleset
- Malware detection software is installed
- Cron jobs run the scanners in set intervals
- The mailing subsystem is configured to make sure the cron jobs can deliver their output

There are two general ways you can go about the task of creating a class of this magnitude. It can either become what one might call a **monolithic** implementation—a class with a large body that comprises all resources that work together to form the desired security baseline. On the other hand, you could aim for a **composite** design, with few resources (or none at all) in the class body and a number of include statements for simpler classes instead. The functionality is compartmentalized, and the central class acts as a collector.

We have not yet touched on the ability of classes to include other classes. That's because it's quite simple. The body of a class can comprise almost any manifest, and the include statement is no exception. Among the few things that cannot appear in a class are node blocks.

 A class can even contain the definition of another class or a defined type. This works *only* in classes, not in defines. There is a dedicated section about this nesting option later in this chapter.

Adding some life to the descriptions, this is how the respective classes will roughly look like:

```
class monolithic_security {
    package {
        [ 'iptables', 'rkhunter', 'postfix' ]:
            ensure => 'installed';
    }
    cron {
        'run-rkhunter':
            ...
    }
    file {
        '/etc/init.d/iptables-firewall':
            source => ...
            mode   => 755;
        '/etc/postfix/main.cf':
            ensure  => 'file',
            content => ...
    }
    service {
        [ 'postfix', 'iptables-firewall' ]:
            ensure => 'running',
            enable => true;
    }
}

class divided_security {
    include iptables_firewall
    include rkhunter
    include postfix
}
```

When developing your own functional classes, you should not try to pick either of these extremes. Most classes will end up anywhere on the spectrum in between. The choice can be largely based on your personal preference. The technical implications are subtle, but these are the respective drawbacks:

- Consequently aiming for monolithic classes opens you up to resource clashes, because you take almost no advantage of the singleton nature of classes

- Splitting up classes too much can make it difficult to impose order and distribute refresh events—you can refer to the *Establishing relationships among containers* section later in this chapter

Neither of these aspects is of critical importance at many times. The case-by-case design choices will be based on each author's experience and personal preference. When in doubt, lean towards composite designs at first.

Writing component classes

There is another common use case for classes. Instead of filling a class with lots of aspects that work together to achieve a complex goal, you can also limit the class to a very specific purpose. Some classes will contain but one resource. The class wraps the resource, so to speak.

This is useful for resources that are needed in different contexts. By wrapping them away in a class, you can make sure that those contexts do not create multiple declarations of the same resource.

For example, the netcat package can be useful to firewall servers, but also to web application servers. There is probably a firewall class and an appserver class. Both declare the netcat package:

```
package {
    'netcat':
        ensure => 'installed';
}
```

If any server ever has both roles (this might happen for budget reasons or in other unforeseen circumstances), this is a problem: when both the firewall and appserver classes are included, then the resulting manifest declares the netcat package twice. This is forbidden. To resolve this situation, the package resource can be wrapped in a netcat class, which is included by both the firewall and appserver classes:

```
class netcat {
    package {
        'netcat':
            ensure => 'installed';
    }
}
```

Let's consider another typical example for component classes that ensures the presence of some common file path. Assume your IT policy requires all custom scripts and applications to be installed in /opt/company/bin. Many classes (such as firewall and appserver from the previous example) will need some relevant content there. Each class needs to make sure that the directories exist before a script can be deployed inside it. This will be implemented by including a component class that wraps the file resources of the directory tree:

```
class scripts_directory {
    file {
        [ '/opt/company/',
          '/opt/company/bin' ]:
            ensure => 'directory',
            owner  => 'root',
            group  => 'root',
            mode   => '644',
    }
}
```

The component class is a pretty precise concept. However, as you have seen in the previous section about the more powerful classes, the whole range of possible class designs forms a fine-grained scale between the presented examples. All manifests you write will likely comprise more than a few classes. The best way to get a feeling for the best practices is to just go ahead and use classes to build the manifests you need.

> The terms **comprehensive** class and **component** class are not official Puppet language and the community does not use them to communicate design practices. I chose them arbitrarily to describe the ideas I laid out in these sections. The same holds true for the descriptions of the use cases for defined types, which will be seen in the next sections.

Next, let's look at some uses for defined types.

Using defined types as resource wrappers

For all their apparent similarity to classes, defined types are used in different ways. For example, the component class was described as *wrapping a resource*. This is accurate in a very specific context—the wrapped resource is a singleton, and it can only appear in one form throughout the manifest.

When wrapping a resource in a defined type instead, you end up with a variation on the respective resource type. The manifest can contain an arbitrary number of instances of the defined type, and each will wrap a distinct resource.

For this to work, the name of the resource that is declared in the body of the defined type must be dynamically created. It is almost always the $name variable of the respective defined type instance, or a value derived from it.

Here is yet another typical example from the many manifests out there: most users who make use of Puppet's file serving capabilities will want to wrap the `file` type at some point so that the respective URL need not be typed for each file:

```
define module_file($module) {
    file {
        $name:
            source => "puppet:///modules/$module/$name"
    }
}
```

This makes it easy to get Puppet to sync files from the master to the agent. The master copy must be properly placed in the named modules on the master:

```
module_file {
    '/etc/ntpd.conf':
        module => 'ntp';
}
```

This resource will make Puppet retrieve the `ntp.conf` file from the `ntp` module. The preceding declaration is more concise and less redundant than the fully written file resource with the Puppet URL (especially for the large number of files you might need to synchronize), which would resemble the following:

```
file {
    '/etc/ntpd.conf':
        source => 'puppet:///modules/ntp/etc/ntpd.conf';
}
```

For a wrapper such as `module_file`, which will likely be used very widely, you will want to make sure that it supports all attributes of the wrapped resource type. In this case, the `module_file` wrapper should accept all `file` attributes. For example, this is how you add the `mode` attribute to the wrapper type:

```
define module_file($module,
                    $mode = undef) {
    if $mode != undef { File { mode => $mode } }
    file {
        $name:
```

```
                    source => "puppet:///modules/$module/$name"
    }
}
```

The `File { ... }` block declares some default values for all `file` resource attributes in the same scope. The `undef` value is similar to Ruby's `nil` and is a convenient parameter default value, because it is very unlikely that a user will need to pass it as an actual value for the wrapped resource. Inlining the whole `if` block is usually a bad practice, but it can ease maintenance in this case, if you end up supporting a lot of parameters this way.

> You can employ the override syntax instead of the default syntax as well:
>
> ```
> File[$name] { mode => $mode }
> ```
>
> This makes the intent of the code slightly more obvious, but is not necessary in the presence of just one `file` resource. *Chapter 6, Leveraging the Full Toolset of the Language*, holds more information about overrides and defaults.

Using defined types as resource multiplexers

Wrapping single resources with a defined type is really useful, but sometimes you will want to add functionality beyond the resource type you are wrapping. At other times, you might wish for your defined type to unify a lot of functionality, just like the comprehensive classes from the beginning of the section.

For both scenarios, what you want to have is multiple resources in the body of your defined type. There is a classic example for this as well:

```
define user_with_key($key,
                     $uid = undef,
                     $group = 'users') {
    if $uid != undef { User { uid => $uid } }
    user {
        $title:
            gid        => $group,
            managehome => true,
    }
    ->
    ssh_authorized_key {
        "key_for_$title":
            ensure => present,
            user   => $title,
```

```
        type   => 'rsa',
        key    => $key,
      }
  }
```

This code allows you to create user accounts with authorized SSH keys in one resource declaration. This code sample has some notable aspects:

- Since you are essentially wrapping multiple resource types, the titles of all *inner* resources are derived from the instance title (or name) of the current defined type instance; actually, this is a safe practice for all defined types
- You can hardcode parts of your business logic; in this example, we dispensed with the support for non-RSA SSH keys and define users as the default group
- Resources inside defined types can and should manage ordering among themselves (using the chaining arrow - > in this case)

Using defined types as macros

Some source code requires many repetitive tasks. Assume that your site uses a subsystem that relies on symbolic links at a certain location to enable configuration files, just like init does with the symlinks in rc2.d/ and its siblings, which point back to ../init.d/<service>.

A manifest that enables a large number of configuration snippets might look like this:

```
file {
    '/etc/example_app/conf.d.enabled/england':
        ensure => 'link',
        target => '../conf.d.available/england';
    '/etc/example_app/conf.d.enabled/ireland':
        ensure => 'link',
        target => '../conf.d.available/ireland';
    '/etc/example_app/conf.d.enabled/germany':
        ensure => 'link',
        target => '../conf.d.available/germany';
    ...
}
```

This is tiring to read and somewhat painful to maintain. In a C program, one would use a preprocessor macro that just takes the base name of both link and target and expands to the three lines of each resource description. Puppet does not use a preprocessor, but you can use defined types to achieve a similar result:

```
define example_app_config {
    file {
        "/etc/example_app/conf.d.enabled/$name":
            ensure => 'link',
            target => "../conf.d.available/$name",
    }
}
```

 The defined type actually acts more like a simple function call than an actual macro.

The define requires no arguments—it can rely solely on its resource name, so the preceding code can now be simplified to the following:

```
example_app_config {
    'england': ;
    'ireland': ;
    'germany': ;
    ...
}
```

Alternatively, the following code is even more terse:

```
example_app_config {
    [ 'england', 'ireland', 'germany', ... ]:
}
```

This array notation leads us to another important use of defined types.

Exploiting array values using defined types

One of the more common scenarios in programming is the requirement to accept an array value from some source and perform some task on each value. Puppet manifests are not exempt from this.

Let's assume that the symbolic links from the previous example actually led to directories and that each such directory would hold a subdirectory to hold optional links to regions. Puppet should manage those links as well.

Of course, after learning about the macro aspect of defined types, you would not want to add each of those regions as distinct resources to your manifest. However, you will need to devise a way to map region names to countries. Seeing as there is already a defined resource type for countries, there is a very direct approach to this: make the list of regions an attribute (or rather, a parameter) of the defined type:

```
define example_app_config($regions = []) {
    file {
        "/etc/example_app/conf.d.enabled/$name":
            ensure => 'link',
            target => "../conf.d.available/$name",
    }
    # to do: add functionality for $regions
}
```

Using the parameter is straightforward:

```
example_app_config {
    'england': regions => [ 'South East', 'London' ];
    'ireland': regions => [ 'Connacht', 'Ulster' ];
    'germany': regions => [ 'Berlin', 'Bayern', 'Hamburg' ];
    ...
}
```

The actual challenge is putting these values to use. A naïve approach is to add the following to the definition of example_app_config:

```
file { $regions:
    path    =>
        "/etc/example_app/conf.d.enabled/$title/regions/$name",
    ensure => 'link',
    target => "../../regions.available/$name";
}
```

However, this will not work. The $name variable does not refer to the title of the file resource that is being declared. It actually refers (just like $title) to the name of the enclosing class or defined type (in this case, the country name). Still, the construct will seem quite familiar to you. The only missing piece here is yet another defined type:

```
define example_app_region($country) {
    file {
        "/etc/example_app/conf.d.enabled/$country/regions/$name",
            ensure => 'link',
            target => "../../regions.available/$name";
    }
}
```

The complete definition of the `example_app_config` defined type should look like this then:

```
define example_app_config($regions = []) {
    file {
        "/etc/example_app/conf.d.enabled/$name":
            ensure => 'link',
            target => "../conf.d.available/$name",
    }
    example_app_region {
        $regions:
            country => $name
    }
}
```

The *outer* defined type adapts the behavior of the `example_app_region` type to its respective needs by passing its own resource name as a parameter value.

> When you are reading this, Puppet Labs would have probably released Puppet 4 already. This release introduces language features for actual array iteration (such as the `map` function). These features are available as a technology preview in Puppet 3.4 or higher, when the `parser=future` option is enabled in the master's configuration. (This option should not be used in production environments.)
> This allows you to omit the secondary define:
>
> ```
> define example_app_config($regions = []) {
>     file {
>         "/etc/example_app/conf.d.enabled/$name":
>             ensure => 'link',
>             target => "../conf.d.available/$name",
>     }
>     map($regions) |$region| {
>         $path = '/etc/example_app/conf.d.enabled/'
>         file {
>             "$path/$name/regions/$region",
>                 ensure => 'link',
>                 target => "../../regions.
> available/$region";
>         }
>     }
> }
> ```
>
> (The $path variable has been introduced to avoid a very long line for the file name.)

Note that if you want the countries to be stored in an array as well, or need another layer of data that is mapped to each region, this pattern will not suffice. I will not go into this problem here, because it is beside the point of how defined types work. *Chapter 7, Separating Data from Code Using Hiera*, discusses structured data and how to use it efficiently.

Including classes from defined types

The `example_app_config` type that was defined in the previous example is supposed to serve a very specific purpose. Therefore, it assumes that the base directory, `/etc/example_app`, and its subdirectories were managed independently, outside the defined type. This was a sound design, but many defined types are meant to be used from lots of independent classes or other defined types. Such defines need to be self-contained.

In our example, the defined type needs to make sure that the following resources are part of the manifest:

```
file {
    [ '/etc/example_app',
      '/etc/example_app/config.d.enabled' ]:
        ensure => 'directory';
}
```

Just putting this declaration into the body of the define will lead to duplicate resource errors. Each instance of `example_app_config` will try to declare the directories by itself. However, we already discussed a pattern to avoid just that issue—I called it the component class.

To make sure that any instance of the `example_app_config` type is self-contained and works on its own, wrap the preceding declaration in a class (for example, `class example_app_config_directories`) and make sure to include this class right in the body of the define:

```
define example_app_config($regions = []) {
    include example_app_config_directories
    ...
}
```

 You can refer to the examples that come with your copy of this book for the definition of the class.

Nesting definitions in classes

A somewhat obscure feature of the language is the nesting of containers inside class bodies. Both classes and defined types can be part of a class body. This allows the nested container to access variables that are local to the enclosing class:

```
class example_app {
    $config_dir = '/etc/example_app'
    define symlink {
        "$config_dir/conf.d.enabled/$name":
            ensure => 'link',
            target => "../conf.d.available/$name",
    }
    ...
}
```

Even without a (contrived) shared variable, it is actually not a bad idea to define such macro-style types right in the class that makes exclusive use of them.

> It is important to realize that this does not protect the defined type from invocation anywhere else in your manifest. Puppet has no concept of `private` class elements.

Nesting things in a class creates an implicit namespace. The `symlink` define can be used from outside the class by referencing it like this:

```
example_app::symlink { 'title': ... }
```

This might appear to be a neat way to bring more structure into your manifest code. However, you actually don't need to nest definitions into classes to achieve this; you can just use the double colons in the names of classes and defined types that you create as usual, on the top level of the manifest (which is to say, not inside any class's body).

> This code can have semantic significance, because the : : (double colon) notation does have meaning with respect to namespaces. The next chapter will cover this in more detail, when covering modules and their structure.

To define a simple rule of thumb, use the nesting of containers in a class only if the nested object is closely related to the enclosing class in terms of functionality, and if either of the following is the case:

- The nested class or defined type is very simple, comprising perhaps only one or two lines of manifest code
- The nested object needs access to a local variable value from the enclosing class

Otherwise, it's a sound practice to refrain from nesting, because it tends to impact code readability.

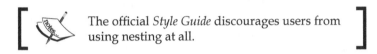 The official *Style Guide* discourages users from using nesting at all.

Establishing relationships among containers

Puppet's classes bear little to no similarity to classes you find in object-oriented programming languages such as Java or Ruby. There are no methods or attributes. You cannot create interfaces or abstract base classes. One of the few shared characteristics is the encapsulation aspect. Just as classes from OOP, Puppet's classes hide implementation details; to get Puppet to start managing a subsystem, you just need to include the appropriate class.

Passing events between classes and defined types

By sorting all resources into classes, you make it unnecessary (for your co-workers or other collaborators) to know about each single resource. This is beneficial. You can think of the collection of classes and defined types as your interface. You would not want to read all manifests that anyone on your project ever wrote.

However, the encapsulation is inconvenient for passing resource events. Say you have some daemon that creates live statistics from your Apache logfiles. It should subscribe to Apache's configuration files so that it can restart if there are any changes (which might be of consequence to this daemon's operation). In another scenario, you might have Puppet manage some external data for a self-compiled Apache module. If Puppet updates such data, you will want to trigger a restart of the Apache service to reload everything.

Armed with the knowledge that there is a `Service['apache2']` defined somewhere in the `apache` class, you can just go ahead and have your module data files notify that resource. It would work—Puppet does not apply any sort of protection to resources that are declared in foreign classes. However, it would pose a minor maintainability issue.

The reference to the resource is located far from the resource itself. When maintaining the manifest later, you or a coworker might wish to look at the resource when encountering the reference. In the case of Apache, it's not difficult to figure out where to look, but in other scenarios, the location of the reference target can be less obvious.

> Looking up a targeted resource is usually not necessary, but it can be important to find out what that resource actually does. It gets especially important during debugging, if after a change to the manifest, the referenced resource is no longer found.

Besides, this approach will not work for the other scenario, in which your daemon needs to subscribe to configuration changes. You could blindly subscribe the central `apache2.conf` file, of course. However, this would not yield the desired results if the responsible class opted to do most of the configuration work inside snippets in `/etc/apache2/conf.d`.

Both scenarios can be addressed cleanly and elegantly by directing the `notify` or `subscribe` parameter at the whole class that is managing the entity in question:

```
file {
    '/var/lib/apache2/sample-module/data01.bin':
        source => '…',
        notify => Class['apache'];
}

service {
    'apache-logwatch':
        enable    => true,
        subscribe => Class['apache'],
}
```

Of course, the signals are now sent (or received) indiscriminately—the file not only notifies `Service['apache2']`, but also every other resource in the `apache` class. This is usually acceptable, because most resources ignore events.

As for the `logwatch` daemon, it might refresh itself needlessly if some resource in the `apache` class needs a sync action. The odds for this occurrence depend on the implementation of the class. For ideal results, it might be sensible to relocate the configuration file resources into their own class so that the daemon can subscribe to that instead.

With your defined types, you can apply the same rules: subscribe to and notify them as required. Doing so feels quite natural, because they are declared like native resources, anyway. This is how you subscribe several instances of a defined type, `symlink`:

```
$active_countries = [ 'England', 'Ireland', 'Germany' ]
service {
    "example-app":
        enable => true,
        subscribe => Symlink[$active_countries];
}
```

Granted, this very example is a bit awkward, because it requires all `symlink` resource titles to be available in an array variable. In this case, it would be more natural to make the defined type instances notify the service instead:

```
symlink {
    [ 'England',
      'Ireland',
      'Germany' ]:
        notify => Service['example-app'],
}
```

This notation passes a metaparameter to a defined type. The result is that this parameter value is applied to all resources declared inside the define.

If a defined type wraps or contains a `service` or `exec` type resource, it can also be desirable to notify an instance of that define to refresh the contained resource. The following example assumes that the `service` type is wrapped by a define type called `protected_service`:

```
file {
    '/etc/example_app/main.conf':
        source => '...',
        notify => Protected_service['example-app'],
}
```

Ordering containers

The `notify` and `subscribe` metaparameters are not the only ones that you can direct at classes and instances of defined types—the same holds true for their siblings `before` and `require`. These allow you to define an order for your resources relative to classes, order instances of your defined types, and even order classes among themselves.

The latter works by virtue of the chaining operator:

```
include firewall
include loadbalancing
Class['firewall'] -> Class['loadbalancing']
```

The effect of this code is that all resources from the `firewall` class will be synchronized before any resource from the `loadbalancing` class, and failure of any resource in the former class will prevent any resource in the latter from being synchronized.

 Note that the chaining arrow cannot just be placed in between the `include` statements. It works only between resources or references.

Because of these ordering semantics, it is actually quite wholesome to require a whole class. You effectively mark the resource in question as being dependent on the class. As a result, it will only be synchronized if the entire subsystem that the class models is successfully synchronized first.

Limitations

Sadly, there is a rather substantial issue with both the ordering of containers and the distribution of refresh events: both will not transcend the `include` statements of further classes. Consider the following example:

```
class apache {
    include apache::service
    include apache::package
    include apache::config
}
file {
    '/etc/apache2/conf.d/passwords.conf':
        source  => '...',
        require => Class['apache'],
}
```

I often mentioned how the comprehensive `class apache` models everything about the Apache server subsystem, and in the previous section, I went on to explain that directing a `require` parameter at such a class will make sure that Puppet only touches the dependent resource if the subsystem has been successfully configured.

This is mostly true, but due to the limitation concerning class boundaries, it doesn't achieve the desired effect in this scenario. The dependent configuration file should actually require the `Package['apache']`, declared in `class apache::package`. However, the relationship does not span multiple class inclusions, so this particular dependency will not be part of the resulting catalog at all.

Similarly, any refresh events sent to the `apache` class will have no effect — they are distributed to resources declared in the class's body (of which there are none), but are not passed on to included classes. Subscribing to the class will make no sense either, because any resource events generated inside included classes will not be forwarded by the `apache` class.

The bottom line is that relationships to classes cannot be built in utter ignorance of their implementation. If in doubt, you need to make sure that the resources that are of interest are actually declared directly inside the class you are targeting.

 The discussion revolved around the example of the `include` statements in classes, but since it is common to use them in defined types as well, the same limitation applies in this case, too.

There is a bright side to this as well. A more correct implementation of the Apache configuration file from the example explained would depend on the package, but synchronize itself before the service, perhaps even notify it (so that Apache restarts if necessary). When all resources are part of the `apache` class and you want to adhere to the pattern of interacting with the container only, this would lead to the following declaration:

```
file {
    '/etc/apache2/conf.d/passwords.conf':
        source  => '…',
        require => Class['apache'],
        notify  => Class['apache'],
}
```

This forms an instant dependency circle: the `file` resource requires all parts of the `apache` class to be synchronized before it gets processed, but to notify them, they must all be put after the `file` resource in the order graph. This cannot work. With the knowledge of the inner structure of the `apache` class, the user can pick metaparameter values that actually work:

```
file {
    '/etc/apache2/conf.d/passwords.conf':
        source  => '...',
        require => Class['apache::package'],
        notify  => Class['apache::service'],
}
```

For the curious, this is what the inner classes look like:

```
class apache::service {
    service {
        'apache2':
            ensure => 'running',
            enable => true,
    }
}
class apache::package {
    package {
        'apache2':
            ensure => 'installed'
    }
}
class apache::config {
    file {
        '/etc/apache2/apache2.conf':
            source => '...',
            mode   => '644',
            notify => Class['apache::service'],
            require => Class['apache::package'],
    }
}
```

The other good news is that invoking defined types does not pose the same kind of issue that an `include` statement of a class does. Events are passed to resources inside defined types just fine, transcending an arbitrary number of stacked invocation. Ordering also works just as expected. Let's keep the example brief:

```
class apache {
    virtual_host {
```

```
        'example.net': ...
    }
    ...
}
```

This `apache` class also creates a virtual host using a defined type. A resource that requires this class will implicitly require all resources from within this `virtual_host` instance. A subscriber to the class will receive events from those resources, and events directed at the class will reach the resources of this `virtual_host`.

There is actually a good reason to make the `include` statements behave differently in that regard. As classes can be included very generously (thanks to their singleton aspect), it is common for classes to build a vast network of includes. By adding a single `include` statement to a manifest, you might unknowingly pull hundreds of classes into this manifest.

If relationships and events transcend this whole network, all manners of unintended effects would be the consequence. Dependency circles will be nearly inevitable. The whole construct will become utterly unmanageable. The cost of such relationships will also grow exponentially — refer to the next section.

Performance implications of container relationships

There is another aspect that you should keep in mind whenever you are referencing a container type to build a relationship to it. The Puppet agent will have to build a dependency graph from this. This graph contains all resources as nodes and all relationships as edges. Classes and defined types get expanded to all their declared resources. All relationships to the container are expanded to relationships to each resource.

This is mostly harmless if the other end of the relationship is a native resource. A file that requires a class with five declared resources leads to five dependencies. That does not hurt. It gets more interesting if the same class is required by an instance of a defined type that comprises three resources. Each of these builds a relationship to each of the class' resources, so you end up with 15 edges in the graph.

It gets even more expensive when a container invokes complex defined types, perhaps even recursively.

A more complex graph means more work for the Puppet agent, and its runs will take longer. This is especially annoying when running agents interactively during debugging or development of your manifest. To avoid the unnecessary effort, consider your relationship declarations carefully and use them only when they are really appropriate.

Mitigating the limitations

The architects of the Puppet language have devised two alternative approaches to solve the ordering issues. We will consider both, because you might encounter them in existing manifest. In new setups, you should always choose the latter variant.

The anchor pattern

The anchor pattern is the classic workaround for the problem with ordering and signaling in the context of recursive class include statements. It can be illustrated by the following example class:

```
class example_app {
    anchor {
        'example_app::begin':
            notify => Class['example_app_config'];
    }
    include exampe_app_config
    anchor {
        'example_app::end':
            require => Class['example_app_config']
    }
}
```

Consider a resource that is placed before => Class['example_app']. It ends up in the chain before each anchor, and therefore, also before any resource in example_app_config, despite the include limitation. This is because the Anchor['example_app::begin'] pseudo-resource notifies the included class and is therefore ordered before all of its resources. A similar effect works for objects that require the class, by virtue of the example::end anchor.

The anchor resource type was created for this express purpose. It is not part of the Puppet core, but has been made available through the stdlib module instead. Since it also forwards refresh events, it is even possible to notify and subscribe this anchored class, and events will propagate into and out of the included class example_app_config.

The `stdlib` module is available from the Puppet Forge, but more about this in the next chapter. There is a descriptive document for the `anchor` pattern to be found online as well, in Puppet Labs' Redmine issue tracker (now obsolete) at (`http://projects.puppetlabs.com/projects/puppet/wiki/Anchor_Pattern`). It is somewhat dated, seeing as the anchor pattern has been supplanted as well by Puppet's ability to contain a class in a container.

The contain function

To make composite classes directly work around the limitations of the `include` statement, you can take advantage of the `contain` function found in Puppet Version 3.4.x or newer.

If the earlier `apache` example had been written like the following, there would have been no issues concerning ordering and refresh events:

```
class apache {
    contain apache::service
    contain apache::package
    contain apache::config
}
```

The official documentation describes the behavior as follows:

> *"A contained class will not be applied before the containing class is begun, and will be finished before the containing class is finished."*

This might read like we're now discussing the panacea for the presented class ordering issues here. Should you just be using `contain` in place of `include` from here on out and never worry about class ordering again? Of course not, this would introduce lots of unnecessary ordering constraints and lead you into unfixable dependency circles very quickly. Do contain classes, but make sure that it makes sense. The contained class should really form a vital part of what the containing class is modeling.

 The quoted documentation refers to classes as containers only, but classes can be contained in defined types just as well. The effect of containment is not limited to ordering aspects either. Refresh events are also correctly propagated.

Making classes more flexible through parameters

Up until this point, classes and defines were presented as direct opposites with respect to flexibility; defined types are inherently adaptable through different parameter values, whereas classes model just one static piece of state. As the section title suggests, this is not entirely true. Classes too can have parameters. Their definition and declaration become rather similar to those of defined types in this case:

```
class apache::config($max_clients=100) {
    file {
        '/etc/apache2/conf.d/max_clients.conf':
            content => "MaxClients $max_clients\n"
    }
}
class {
    'apache::config':
        max_clients => 120;
}
```

This enables some very elegant designs, but introduces some drawbacks as well.

Caveats of parameterized classes

The consequence of allowing class parameters is almost obvious: you lose the singleton characteristic. Well, that's not entirely true either, but your freedom in declaring the class gets limited drastically.

Classes that define default values for all parameters can still be declared with the `include` statement. This can still be done an arbitrary number of times in the same manifest.

However, the resource-like declaration of class { 'name': } cannot appear more than once for any given class in the same manifest. This is in keeping with the rules for resources and should not be very surprising—after all, it would be very awkward to try and bind different values to a class' parameters in different locations throughout the manifest.

Things become very confusing when mixing include with the alternative syntax though. It is valid to include a class an arbitrary number of times after it has been declared using the resource-like notation. However, you cannot use the resource style declaration *after* a class has been declared using include. That's because the parameters are then determined to assume their default values and a class { 'name': } declaration clashes with that.

In a nutshell, the following code works:

```
class { 'apache::config': }
include apache::config
```

However, the following code does not work:

```
include apache::config
class { 'apache::config': }
```

As a consequence, you effectively cannot add parameters to component classes, because the include statement is no longer safe to use in large quantities. Therefore, parameters are essentially only useful for comprehensive classes, which usually don't get included from different parts of the manifest.

> *Chapter 5*, *Extending Your Puppet Infrastructure with Modules*, will discuss some alternate patterns, some of which exploit class parameters. Also note that *Chapter 7*, *Separating Data from Code Using Hiera*, presents you with a solution that gives you more flexibility with parameterized classes. Using this, you can be more liberal with your class interfaces.

Preferring the include keyword

Ever since class parameters have been available, some Puppet users have felt compelled to write (example) code that would make it a point to forgo the include keyword in favor of resource-like class declarations, such as this:

```
class apache {
    class { 'apache::service': }
    class { 'apache::package': }
    class { 'apache::config': }
}
```

Doing this is a very bad idea. I cannot stress this enough: one of the most powerful concepts about Puppet's classes is their singleton aspect—the ability to include a class in a manifest arbitrarily and without worrying about clashes with other code. The mentioned declaration syntax deprives you of this power, even when the classes in question don't even support parameters.

The safest route is to use `include` whenever possible and to avoid the alternate syntax whenever you can. In fact, *Chapter 7, Separating Data from Code Using Hiera*, introduces the ability to use class parameters without the resource-like class declaration. This way, you can rely solely on `include`, even when parameters are in play. These are the safest recommended practices to keep you out of trouble from incompatible class declarations.

Summary

Classes and defined types are the essential tools to create reusable Puppet code. While classes hold resources that must not be repeated in a manifest, the define is capable of managing a distinct set of adapted resources upon every invocation. It does that by leveraging the parameter values it receives. While classes do support parameters as well, there are some caveats to bear in mind.

To use defined types in your manifest, you declare instances just like resources of native types. Classes are mainly used through the `include` statement, although there are alternatives such as the `class { }` syntax or the `contain` function.

There are also some ordering issues with classes that the `contain` function can help mitigate.

In theory, classes and defines suffice to build almost all manifests that you will ever need. In practice, you will want to organize your code into larger structures. The next chapter will show you how to do exactly that and a whole range of useful functionality beyond it.

5
Extending Your Puppet Infrastructure with Modules

In the previous chapter, you learned about the tools that create modularized and reusable Puppet code in the form of classes and defined types. We discussed that almost all Puppet resources should be separated into appropriate classes, except if they logically need to be part of a defined type. This is almost enough syntax to build manifests for an entire fleet of agent nodes—each selecting the appropriate composite classes, which in turn include further required classes, with all classes recursively instantiating defined types.

What has not been discussed up until now is the organization of manifests in the filesystem. It is obviously undesirable to stuff all of your code into a large `site.pp` file. The answer to this problem is provided by modules and will be explained in this chapter.

Besides organizing classes and defines, modules are also a way to share common code. They are software libraries for Puppet manifests and plugins. They also offer a convenient place to locate the interface descriptions that were hinted at in the previous chapter.

The existence and general location of modules were mentioned briefly in *Chapter 3, A Peek Under the Hood – Facts, Types, and Providers*. It is now time to explore these and other aspects in greater detail. We'll cover the following topics in this chapter:

- An overview of Puppet's modules
- Maintaining environments
- Following modules' best practices
- Building a specific module
- Finding helpful Forge modules

An overview of Puppet's modules

A module can be seen as a higher-order organizational unit. It bundles up classes and defined types that contribute to a common management goal (specific system aspects or a piece of software, for example). These manifests are not all that is organized through modules—most modules also bundle files and file templates. There can also be several kinds of Puppet plugins in a module. This section will explain these different parts of a module and show you where they are located. You will also learn about the means of module documentation and how to obtain existing modules for your own use.

Parts of a module

For most modules, **manifests** form the most important part—the core functionality. The manifests consist of classes and defined types, which all share a namespace, rooted at the module name. For example, an `ntp` module will contain only classes and defines whose names start with the `ntp::` prefix.

Many modules will contain files that can be synced to the agent's filesystem. This is often used for configuration files or snippets. You have seen examples of this, but let's repeat them. A frequent occurrence in many manifests are `file` resources such as the following:

```
file {
    '/etc/ntp.conf':
        source => 'puppet:///modules/ntp/ntp.conf',
}
```

There is often a need to tweak some parameters inside such a file so that node manifests can declare customized config settings for the respective agent. The tool of choice for this are templates, which will be discussed in the next chapter.

Another possible component of a module that you have already read about are custom facts—code that gets synchronized to the agent and runs before a catalog is requested so that the output becomes available as facts about the agent system.

These facts are not the only Puppet plugins that can be shipped with modules. There are also **parser functions** (also called **custom functions**), for one. These are actual functions that you can use in your manifests. In many situations, they are the most convenient way, if not the only way, to build some specific implementations.

The final plugin type has also been hinted at in an earlier chapter—custom native types and providers are conveniently placed in modules as well.

How the content of each module is structured

All the mentioned components need to be located in specific filesystem locations for the master to pick them up. Each module forms a directory tree. Its root is named after the module itself. For example, the `ntp` module is stored in a directory called `ntp/`.

All manifests are stored in a subdirectory called `manifests/`. Each class and defined type has its own respective file. The `ntp::package` class will be found in `manifests/package.pp`, and the defined type called `ntp::monitoring::nagios`, will be found in `manifests/monitoring/nagios.pp`. The first particle of the container name (`ntp`) is always the module name, and the rest describes the location under `manifests/`. You can refer to the module tree in the following paragraphs for more examples.

The `manifests/init.pp` file is special. It can be thought of as a default manifest location, because it is looked up for any definition from the module in question. Both of the examples that were just mentioned can be put into `init.pp` and will still work. Doing this makes it harder to locate the definitions, though.

In practice, `init.pp` should only hold one class, which is named after the module (such as the `ntp` class), if your module implements such a class. This is a common practice, as it allows manifests to use a simple statement to tap the core functionality of the module:

```
include ntp
```

You can refer to the *Modules' best practices* section for some more notes on this subject.

The files and templates that a module serves to agents are not as strictly sorted into specific locations. It is only important that they be placed in the `files/` and `templates/` subdirectories, respectively. The contents of these subtrees can be structured to the module author's liking, and the manifest must reference them correctly. Static files should always be addressed through URLs such as these:

```
puppet:///modules/ntp/ntp.conf
puppet:///modules/my_app/opt/scripts/find_my_app.sh
```

These files are found in corresponding subdirectories of `files/`:

```
.../modules/ntp/files/ntp.conf
.../modules/my_app/files/opt/scripts/find_my_app.sh
```

The `modules` prefix in the URI is mandatory and is always followed by the module name. The rest of the path translates directly to contents of the `files/` directory. There are similar rules for templates. You can refer to *Chapter 6, Leveraging the Full Toolset of the Language*, for the details.

Finally, all plugins are located in the `lib/` subtree. Custom facts are Ruby files in `lib/facter/`. Parser functions are stored in `lib/puppet/parser/functions/`, and for custom types and providers, there is `lib/puppet/type/` and `lib/puppet/provider/`, respectively. This is not a coincidence—these Ruby libraries are looked up by the master and the agent in the according namespaces. There are examples for all these components later in this chapter.

In short, these are the contents of a possible module in a tree view:

```
/etc/puppet/environments/production/my_app
   templates       # templates are covered in the next chapter
   files
      subdir1       # puppet:///modules/my_app/subdir1/<filename>
      subdir2       # puppet:///modules/my_app/subdir2/<filename>
         subsubdir  # puppet:///modules/my_app/subdir2/subsubdir/...
   manifests
      init.pp       # class my_app            is defined here
      params.pp     # class my_app::params    is defined here
      config
         detail.pp  # my_app::config::detail  is defined here
         basics.pp  # my_app::config::basics  is defined here
   lib
      facter          # contains .rb files with custom facts
      puppet
         parser
            functions # contains .rb files with parser functions
         type         # contains .rb files with custom types
         provider     # contains .rb files with custom providers
```

Documentation in modules

A module can and should include documentation. The Puppet master does not process any module documentation by itself. As such, it is largely up to the authors to decide how to structure the documentation of modules that are created for their specific site only. That being said, there are some common practices, and it's a good idea to adhere to them. Besides, if a module should end up being published on the Forge, appropriate documentation should be considered mandatory.

 The process of publishing modules is beyond the scope of this book. You can find a guide at `https://docs.puppetlabs.com/puppet/latest/reference/modules_publishing.html`.

For many modules, the main focus of the documentation is centered on the README file, which is located right in the module's root directory. It is customarily formatted in Markdown as README.md or README.markdown. The README file should contain explanations, and often, there is a reference documentation as well.

Puppet DSL interfaces can also be documented right in the manifest, in the rdoc and YARD format. This applies to classes and defined types:

```
# Class: my_app::firewall
## This class adds firewall rules to allow access to my_app.
#
# Parameters: none
class my_app::firewall {
    # class code here
}
```

You can generate HTML documentation (including navigation) for all your modules using the puppet doc subcommand. This practice is somewhat more obscure, so it won't be discussed here in great detail. If this option is attractive to you, I encourage you to peruse the documentation—puppet help doc is a good starting point. Another useful resource is the puppetlabs-strings module (https://forge.puppetlabs.com/puppetlabs/strings).

Plugins are documented right in their Ruby code. There are examples for this in the following sections.

Maintaining environments

Puppet doesn't organize only manifests, files, and plugins in modules. There is a higher-level unit called **environment** that groups and contains modules. An environment mainly consists of:

- One or more site manifest files
- A modules directory

When the master compiles the manifest for a node, it uses exactly one environment for this task. As described in *Chapter 2, The Master and Its Agents*, it always starts in site.pp, which is the environment's site manifest. This can be the location for your node blocks. It is a common practice to keep the node blocks out of site.pp, though, and keep them in a nodes.pp file instead. Before we take a look at how this works, let's see an example environment directory:

```
/etc/puppet/environments
  production
```

```
environment.conf
manifests
   init.pp
   nodes.pp
modules
   my_app
   ntp
```

The `environment.conf` file can customize the environment. This is required if you want to use `nodes.pp` or other files in the `manifests` directory. To make Puppet read all `pp` files in this directory, set the `manifest` option in `environment.conf`:

```
# /etc/puppet/environments/production/environment.conf
manifest = manifests
```

The `nodes.pp` file will include classes and instantiate defines from the modules. Puppet looks for modules in the `modules` subdirectory of the active environment. You can define additional subdirectories in order to hold modules by setting the `modulepath` option in `environment.conf`:

```
# /etc/puppet/environments/production/environment.conf
manifest = manifests
modulepath = modules:site-modules
```

The directory structure can be more distinctive, then:

```
/etc/puppet/environments/
   production
     manifests
     modules
       ntp
     site-modules
       my_app
```

Configuring environment locations

Puppet uses the `production` environment by default. This and other environments should be stored in a dedicated directory, such as `/etc/puppet/environments`, which contains nothing but environment directories. Allow Puppet to detect the named environments there by setting the `environmentpath` option in `puppet.conf`:

```
[main]
environmentpath = /etc/puppet/environments
```

This is a new option introduced in Puppet Version 3.5. Earlier versions would configure environments right in puppet.conf with their respective manifest and modulepath settings. These work just like the settings from environment.conf:

```
# in puppet.conf (Deprecated!)
[testing]
manifest = /etc/puppet/environments/testing/manifests
modulepath = /etc/puppet/environments/testing/modules
```

For the special production environment, these Puppet setups will use the manifest and modulepath settings from the [main] or [master] section. An old default configuration had the production environment look for manifests and modules right in /etc/puppet:

```
# Deprecated! Works only with Puppet 3.x!
[main]
manifest = /etc/puppet/site.pp
modulepath = /etc/puppet/modules
```

Sites that operate like this today should be migrated to the aforementioned directory environments in /etc/puppet/environments or similar locations.

Obtaining and installing modules

Downloading existing modules is very common. Puppet Labs is hosting a dedicated site for sharing and obtaining modules—the Puppet Forge. It works just like RubyGems or CPAN and makes it simple for the user to retrieve a given module through a command-line interface. In the Forge, modules are fully named by prefixing the actual module name with the author, such as puppetlabs-stdlib or ffrank-constraints.

The puppet module install command will install a module in the active environment:

puppet module install puppetlabs-stdlib

 The *Testing your modules* section has information on using different environments.

The current release of the stdlib module (authored by the user, puppetlabs) is downloaded from the Forge and installed in the standard modules location. This is the first location in the current environment's modulepath, which is usually the modules subdirectory.

The stdlib module should be considered mandatory—it adds a large number of useful functions to the Puppet language. Examples include the keys, values, and has_key functions, which are essential for implementing the proper handling of hash structures, to name only a few. The functions are available to your manifests as soon as the module is installed—there is no need to include any class or other explicit loading. If you write your own modules that add functions, these are loaded automatically just the same.

Modules' best practices

With all current versions of Puppet, you should make it a habit to put all the manifest code into modules, with only a few exceptions:

- The node blocks
- The include statements for very select classes that should be omnipresent
- Declarations of helpful variables that should have the same availability as Facter facts in your manifests

This section provides details on how to organize your manifests accordingly. It also advises some design practices and strategies in order to test changes to modules.

Putting everything in modules

You might find some manifests in older installations that gather lots of manifest files in one or more directories and use the import statements in the site.pp file, such as:

```
import '/etc/puppet/manifests/custom/*.pp'
```

All classes and defined types in these files are then available globally.

This whole approach had scalability issues and has long been deprecated. The import keyword is missing from Puppet 4 and newer versions.

It is far more efficient to give meaningful names to classes and defined types so that Puppet can look them up in the collection of modules. The scheme has been discussed in an earlier section already, so let's just look at another example where the Puppet compiler encounters a class name such as:

```
include ntp::server::component::watchdog
```

It will go ahead and locate the `ntp` module in all the configured module locations of the active environment (path names in the `modulepath` setting). It will then try and read the `ntp/manifests/server/component/watchdog.pp` file in order to find the class definition. Failing this, it will also try `ntp/manifests/init.pp`.

This makes compilation very efficient: Puppet dynamically identifies the required manifest files and includes only those for parsing. It also aids code inspection and development, because it is abundantly clear where you should look for specific definitions.

> Technically, it is possible to stuff all of a module's manifests into its `init.pp` file, but you lose the advantages that a structured tree of module manifests offers.

Avoiding generalization

Each module should ideally serve a specific purpose. On a site that relies on Puppet to manage a diverse server infrastructure, there are likely modules for each respective service, such as `apache`, `ssh`, `nagios`, `nginx`, and so forth. There can also be site-specific modules such as `users` or `shell_settings` if operations require this kind of fine-grained control. It might even be sensible to have a module for each individual administrator's user account if each has certain preferences that require rather elaborate manifests.

The ideal granularity depends on the individual requirements of your setup. What you generally want to avoid are modules with names such as `utilities` or `helpers` that serve as a melting pot for ideas that don't fit in any existing modules. Such a lack of organization can be detrimental to discipline and can lead to chaotic modules that include definitions that should have become their own respective modules instead.

Adding more modules is cheap. A module generally incurs no cost for the Puppet master operation, and your user experience will usually become more efficient with more modules, not less so. Of course, this balance can tip if your site imposes a special documentation or other handling prerequisites on each module. Such rulings must then be weighed into the decisions about module organization.

Testing your modules

Depending on the size of your agent network, some or many of your modules can be used by a large variety of nodes. Despite these commonalities, these nodes can be quite different from one another. A change to a central module such as ssh or ntp, which are likely used by a large number of agents, can have quite extensive consequences.

The first and most important tool for testing your work is the --noop option for Puppet. It works for puppet agent as well as puppet apply. If it is given on the command line, Puppet will not perform any necessary sync actions but merely present the respective line of output to you instead. There is an example of this in *Chapter 1, Writing Your First Manifests*.

When using a master instead of working locally with puppet apply, a new problem arises, though. The master is queried by all your agents. Unless all agents are disabled while you are testing a new manifest, it is very likely that one will check in and accidentally run the untested code.

> In fact, even your test agent can trigger its regular run while you are logged in, transparently in the background.

It is very important to guard against such uncontrolled manifest applications. A small mistake can damage a number of agent machines in a short time period. The best way to go about this is to define multiple environments on the master.

Safe testing with environments

Besides the production environment, you should create at least one testing environment. You can call it testing or whatever you like. When using directory environments, just create its directory in the environmentpath. On older versions of Puppet prior to 3.5, add it to puppet.conf:

```
[testing]
manifest=/etc/puppet/environments/testing/manifests
modulepath=/etc/puppet/environments/testing/modules
```

Such an additional environment is very useful for testing changes. The test environment or environments should be copies of the production data. Prepare all manifest changes in testing first. You can make your agents test this change before you copy it to production:

```
puppet agent --test --noop --env testing
```

You can even omit the `noop` flag on some or all of your agents so that the change is actually deployed. Some subtle mistakes in manifests cannot be detected from an inspection of the `noop` output, so it is usually a good idea to run the code at least once before releasing it.

 Environments are even more effective when used in conjunction with source control, especially distributed systems such as `git` or `mercurial`. Versioning your Puppet code is a good idea independently of environments and testing—this is one of the greatest advantages that Puppet has to offer you through its **Infrastructure as Code** paradigm.

Using environments and the `noop` mode form a pragmatic approach to testing that can serve in most scenarios. The safety against erroneous Puppet behavior is limited, of course. There are more formal ways of testing modules:

- The `rspec-puppet` module allows module authors to implement unit tests based on `rspec`. You can find more details at `http://rspec-puppet.com/`.

- Acceptance testing can be performed through `beaker`. You can refer to `https://github.com/puppetlabs/beaker/wiki/How-To-Beaker` for details.

Explaining these tools in detail is beyond the scope of this book.

Building a specific module

This chapter has discussed many theoretical and operational aspects of modules, but you are yet to gain an insight into the process of writing modules. For this purpose, the rest of this chapter will have you create an example module step by step.

It should be stressed again that for the most part, you will want to find general purpose modules from the Forge. The number of available modules is ever growing, so the odds are good that there is something already there to help you with what you need to do.

Assume that you want to add Cacti to your network—an RRDtool-based trend monitor and graphing server, including a web interface. You would first check the Forge and indeed find some modules. However, let's further assume that neither speaks to you—either the feature set or the implementation is not to your liking. If even the respective interfaces don't meet your requirements, it doesn't make much sense to base your own module on an existing one (in the form of a fork on GitHub) either. You will need to write your module from scratch.

Naming your module

Module names should be concise and to the point. If you manage a specific piece of software, name your module after it—apache, java, mysql, and so forth. Avoid verbs such as install_cacti or manage_cacti. If your module name does need to consist of several words (because the target subsystem has a long name), they should be divided by underscore characters. Spaces, dashes, and other non-alphanumeric characters are not allowed.

In our example, the module should just be named cacti.

Making your module available to Puppet

To use your own module, you don't need to make it available for installation through puppet module. For this, you will need to upload the module to the Forge first, which will require quite some additional effort. Luckily, a module will work just fine without all this preparation if you just put the source code in the proper location on your master.

To create your own cacti module, create the basic directories:

```
mkdir -p /etc/puppet/environments/testing/cacti/{manifests,files}
```

Don't forget to synchronize all changes to production once the agents use them.

Implementing the basic module functionality

Most modules will perform all of their work through their manifests.

 There are notable exceptions, such as the stdlib module. It mainly adds parser functions and a few general-purpose resource types.

When planning the classes for your module, it is most straightforward to think about how you would like to use the finished module. There is a wide range of possible interface designs. The de facto standard stipulates that the managed subsystem is initialized on the agent system by including the module's main class—the class that bears the same name as the module and is implemented in the module's init.pp file.

For our Cacti module, the user should use this:

```
include cacti
```

As a result, Puppet should take all the required steps in order to install the software and if necessary, perform any additional initialization.

Start by creating the `cacti` class and implementing the setup in the way you would from the command line, replacing commands with appropriate Puppet resources. On a Debian system, installing the `cacti` package is enough. Other required software is brought in through dependencies (completing the LAMP stack), and after the package installation, the interface becomes available through the web URI `/cacti/` on the server machine:

```
# .../modules/cacti/manifests/init.pp
class cacti {
    package { 'cacti':
        ensure => 'installed'
    }
}
```

Your module is now ready for testing. Invoke it from your agent's manifest in `site.pp` or `nodes.pp` of the `testing` environment:

```
node 'agent' {
    include cacti
}
```

Apply it on your agent directly:

root@agent# puppet agent --test --env testing

This will work on Debian, and Cacti is reachable via `http://<address>/cacti/`. It's unfortunate that the Cacti web interface will not come up when the home page is requested through the `/` URI. To enable this, give the module the ability to configure an appropriate redirection. Prepare an Apache configuration snippet in the module in `/etc/puppet/environments/testing/cacti/files/etc/apache2/conf.d/cacti-redirect.conf`:

```
# Do not edit this file - it is managed by Puppet!
RedirectMatch permanent ^/$ /cacti/
```

 The warning notice is helpful, especially when multiple administrators have access to the Cacti server.

It makes sense to add a dedicated class that will sync this file to the agent machine:

```
# .../modules/cacti/manifests/redirect.pp
class cacti::redirect {
    file {
        '/etc/apache2/conf.d/cacti-redirect.conf':
            ensure  => 'file',
            source  => 'puppet:///modules/cacti/etc/apache2/conf.d/
cacti-redirect.conf',
            require => Package['cacti'];
    }
}
```

> A short file like this can also be managed through the `file` type's
> `content` property instead of `source`:
>
> ```
> $puppet_warning = '# Do not edit - managed by Puppet!'
> $line = 'RedirectMatch permanent ^/$ /cacti/'
> file { '/etc/apache2/conf.d/cacti-redirect.conf':
>     ensure  => 'file',
>     content => "${puppet_warning}\n${line}\n",
> }
> ```
>
> This is more efficient, because the content is part of the catalog, so the
> agent does not need to retrieve the checksum through another request
> to the master.

The module now allows the user to `include cacti::redirect` in order to get
this functionality. This is not a bad interface as such, but this kind of modification
is actually well-suited to become a parameter of the `cacti` class:

```
class cacti($redirect = true ) {
    if $redirect {
        contain cacti::redirect
    }
    package { 'cacti':
        ensure => 'installed'
    }
}
```

The redirect is now installed by default when a manifest uses `include cacti`. If the
web server has other virtual hosts that serve things that are not Cacti, this might be
undesirable. In such cases, the manifest will declare the class with this parameter:

```
class { 'cacti': redirect => false }
```

Speaking of the best practices, most modules will also separate the installation routine into a class of its own. In this case, this is hardly helpful, because the installation status is ensured through a single resource, but let's do it anyway:

```
class cacti( $redirect = true ) {
    contain cacti::install
    if $redirect {
        contain cacti::redirect
    }
}
```

It's sensible to use `contain` here in order to make the Cacti management a solid unit. The `cacti::install` class is put into a separate `install.pp` manifest file:

```
# .../modules/cacti/manifests/install.pp
class cacti::install {
    package { 'cacti':
        ensure => 'installed'
    }
}
```

On Debian, the installation process of the `cacti` package copies another Apache configuration file to `/etc/apache2/conf.d`. Since Puppet performs a normal `apt` installation, this result will be achieved. However, Puppet does not make sure that the configuration *stays* in this desired state.

> There is an actual risk that the configuration might get broken. If the `puppetlabs-apache` module is in use for a given node, it will usually purge any unmanaged configuration files from the `/etc/apache2/` tree. Be very careful when you enable this module for an existing server. Test it in the `noop` mode. If required, amend the manifest to include the existing configuration.

It is prudent to add a `file` resource to the manifest that keeps the configuration snippet in its post-installation state. Usually with Puppet, this will require you to copy the config file contents to the module, just like the redirect configuration is in a file on the master. However, since the Debian package for Cacti includes a copy of the snippet in `/usr/share/doc/cacti/cacti.apache.conf`, we can instruct the agent to sync the actual configuration with that. Perform this in yet another de facto standard for modules—the `config` class:

```
# .../modules/cacti/manifests/config.pp
class cacti::config {
    file {
```

```
            '/etc/apache2/conf.d/cacti.conf':
                mode    => 644,
                source => '/usr/share/doc/cacti/cacti.apache.conf'
        }
    }
```

This class should be contained by the `cacti` class as well. Running the agent again will now have no effect, because the configuration is already in place.

Creating utilities for derived manifests

You have now created several classes that compartmentalize the basic installation and configuration work for your module. Classes lend themselves very well to implement global settings that are relevant for the managed software as a whole.

However, just installing Cacti and making its web interface available is not an especially powerful capability — after all, the module does little beyond what a user can achieve by installing Cacti through the package manager. The much greater pain point with Cacti is that it usually requires configuration via said web interface: adding servers as well as choosing and configuring graphs for each server can be an arduous task and require dozens of clicks per server, depending on the complexity of your graphing needs.

This is where Puppet can be the most helpful. A textual representation of the desired states allows for quick copy-and-paste repetition and name substitution through regular expressions. Better yet, once there is a Puppet interface, users can devise their own defined types in order to save themselves even from the copy and paste work.

Speaking of defined types, they are what is required for your module to allow this type of configuration. Each machine in Cacti's configuration should be an instance of a defined type. The graphs can have their own type as well. On the other hand, depending on how much complexity the graph configuration requires, it might be more useful (and easier to implement) to manage them as arguments for the machine type.

As with the implementation of the classes, the first thing you always need to ask yourself is how this task would be done from the command line.

 Actually, the better question can be what API should you use for this, preferably from Ruby. However, this is only important if you intend to write Puppet plugins — types and providers. We will look into this later in this very chapter.

Cacti comes with a set of CLI scripts. The Debian package makes these available in `/usr/share/cacti/cli`. Let's discover these while we step through the implementation of the Puppet interface. The goals are defined types that will effectively wrap the command-line tools so that Puppet can always maintain the defined configuration state through appropriate queries and update commands.

Adding configuration items

While designing more capabilities for the Cacti module, first comes the capability to register a machine for monitoring—or rather, a **device**, as Cacti itself calls it (network infrastructure such as switches and routers are frequently monitored as well, not only computers). The name for the first defined type should, therefore, be `cacti::device`.

> The same warnings from the *Naming your module* subsection apply—don't give in to the temptation of giving names such as `create_device` or `define_domain` to your type, unless you have very good reasons, such as the removal being impossible. Even then, it's probably better to skip the verb.

The CLI script used to register a device is named `add_device.php`. Its help output readily indicates that it requires two parameters, which are `description` and `ip`. A custom description of an entity is often a good use for the respective Puppet resource's title. The type almost writes itself now:

```
# .../modules/cacti/manifests/device.pp
define cacti::device($ip) {
    $cli = '/usr/share/cacti/cli'
    $options = "--description='$name' --ip='$ip'"
    exec {
        "add-cacti-device-$name":
            command => "$cli/add_device.php $options",
            require => Class[cacti],
    }
}
```

> In practice, it is often unnecessary to use so many variables, but it serves readability with the limited horizontal space of the page.

This `exec` resource gives Puppet the ability to use the CLI to create a new device in the Cacti configuration. Since PHP is among Cacti's requirements, it's sufficient to make the `exec` resource `require` the `cacti` class. Note the use of `$name` not only for the `--description` parameter, but in the resource name for the `exec` resource as well. This ensures that each `cacti::device` instance declares a unique `exec` resource in order to create itself.

This still lacks an important aspect, however. Written as in the given example, this `exec` resource will make the Puppet agent run the CLI script always, under any circumstances. This is incorrect, though — it should only run if the device has not yet been added.

Every `exec` resource should have one of the `creates`, `onlyif`, or `unless` parameters. It defines a query for Puppet to determine the current sync state. The `add_device` call must be made *unless* the device exists already. The query for existing devices must be made through the `add_graphs.php` script (counterintuitively). When called with the `--list-hosts` option, it prints one header line and a table of devices, with the description in the fourth column. The following `unless` query will find the resource in question:

```
$search = "sed 1d | cut -f4- | grep -q '^$name\$'"
exec {
    "add-cacti-device-$name":
        command => "$cli/add_device.php $options",
        path    => '/bin:/usr/bin',
        unless  => "$cli/add_graphs.php --list-hosts | $search",
        require => Class[cacti],
}
```

The `path` parameter is useful, because it allows for calling the core utilities without the respective full path.

> It is a good idea to generally set a standard list of search paths, because some tools will not work with an empty `PATH` environment variable.

The `unless` command will return `0` if the exact resource title is found among the list of devices. The final `$` sign is escaped so that Puppet includes it in the `$search` command string literally.

You can now test your new define by adding the following resource to the agent machine's manifest:

```
# in manifests/nodes.pp
node 'agent' {
```

```
    include cacti
    cacti::device {
        'Puppet test agent (Debian 7)':
            ip => $ipaddress;
    }
}
```

On the next `puppet agent --test` run, you will be notified that the command for adding the device is run. Repeat the run, and Puppet will determine that everything is now already synchronized with the catalog.

Allowing customization

The `add_device.php` script has a range of optional parameters that allow the user to customize the device. The Puppet module should expose these dials as well. Let's pick one and implement it in the `cacti::device` type. Each Cacti device has a `ping_method` that defaults to `tcp`. With the module, we can even superimpose our own defaults over those of the software:

```
define cacti::device($ip, $ping_method='icmp') {
    $cli = '/usr/share/cacti/cli'
    $base_opt = "--description='$name' --ip='$ip'"
    $ping_opt = "--ping_method=$ping_method"
    $options = "$base_opt $ping_opt"
    $search = "sed 1d | cut -f4- | grep -q '^$name\$'"
    exec {
        "add-cacti-device-$name":
            command => "$cli/add_device.php $options",
            path    => '/bin:/usr/bin',
            unless  =>
"$cli/add_graphs.php --list-hosts  | $search",
            require => Class[cacti],
    }
}
```

The module uses a default of `icmp` instead of `tcp`. The value is always passed to the CLI script, whether it was passed to the `cacti::device` instance or not. The parameter default is passed in the latter case.

 If you plan to publish your module, it is more sensible to try and use the same defaults as the managed software whenever possible.

Once you incorporate all the available CLI switches, you have successfully created a Puppet API in order to add devices to your Cacti configuration, giving the user the benefits of easy reproduction, sharing, implicit documentation, simple versioning, and more.

Removing unwanted configuration items

There is still one remaining wrinkle. It is atypical for Puppet types to be unable to remove the entities that they create. As it stands, this is a technical limitation of the CLI that powers your module, because it does not implement a `remove_device` function yet. Such scripts have been made available on the Internet but are not properly a part of Cacti at the time of writing this.

To give the module more functionality, it would make sense to incorporate additional CLI scripts among the module's files. You will put the appropriate file into the right directory under `modules/cacti/files/` and add another `file` resource to the `cacti::install` class:

```
file {
    '/usr/share/cacti/cli/remove_device.php':
        module  => 'cacti',
        mode    => 755,
        source  => 'puppet:///modules/cacti/usr/share/cacti/cli/
remove_device.php',
        require => Package['cacti'],
}
```

You can then add an `ensure` attribute to the `cacti::device` type:

```
define cacti::device($ensure='present',$ip,$ping_method='icmp') {
    $cli = '/usr/share/cacti/cli'
    $search = "sed 1d | cut -f4- | grep -q '^$name\$'"
    case $ensure {
    'present': {
        # existing cacti::device code goes here
    }
    'absent': {
        $remove = "$cli/remove_device.php"
        $get_id = "$remove --list-devices
                    | awk -F'\\t' '\$4==\"$name\" { print \$1 }'"
        exec {
            "remove-cacti-device-$name":
                command => "$remove --device-id=\$( $get_id )",
                path    => '/bin:/usr/bin',
```

```
        onlyif  => "$cli/add_graphs.php --list-hosts
                                            | $search",
        require => Class[cacti],
      }
    }
  }
}
```

Note that I took some liberties with the indentation here so as to not break too many lines. This new `exec` resource is quite a mouthful, because the `remove_device.php` script requires the numeric ID of the device to be removed. This is retrieved with a `--list-devices` call that is piped to `awk`. To impair readability even more, some things must be escaped so that Puppet includes a valid `awk` script in the catalog — double quotes, $ signs, and backslashes. Also note that the query for the sync state of this `exec` resource is identical to the one for the `add` resource, except that now it is used with the `onlyif` parameter: *only* take action *if* the device in question is still found in the configuration.

Dealing with complexity

The commands we implemented for the `cacti::device` define are quite convoluted. At this level of complexity, shell one-liners become unwieldy for powering Puppet's resources. It gets even worse when handling graphs — the `add_graphs.php` CLI script requires numeric IDs not only of the devices, but of the graphs as well. At this point, it makes sense to move the complexity out of the manifest and write wrapper scripts for the actual CLI. I will just sketch the implementation. The wrapper script will follow this general pattern:

```
#!/bin/bash
DEVICE_DESCR=$1
GRAPH_DESCR=$2
DEVICE_ID=` #scriptlet to retrieve numeric device ID`
GRAPH_ID=` #scriptlet to retrieve numeric graph ID`
GRAPH_TYPE=`#scriptlet to determine the graph type`
/usr/share/cacti/cli/add_graphs.php \
  --graph-type=$GRAPH_TYPE \
  --graph-template-id=$GRAPH_ID \
  --host-id=$DEVICE_ID
```

With this, you can add a straightforward `graph` type:

```
define cacti::graph($device,$graph=$name) {
    $add = '/usr/local/bin/cacti-add-graph'
    $find = '/usr/local/bin/cacti-find-graph'
```

```
exec {
    "add-graph-$name-to-$device":
        command => "$add '$device' '$graph'",
        path    => '/bin:/usr/bin',
        unless  => "$find '$device' '$graph'",
    }
}
```

This also requires an additional `cacti-find-graph` script. Adding this poses an additional challenge, because the current CLI has no capabilities for listing configured graphs. There are many more functionalities that can be added to a `cacti` module, such as the management of Cacti's data sources and the ability to change options of devices and, possibly, other objects that already exist in the configuration.

Such commodities are beyond the essentials and won't be detailed here. Let's look at some other parts for your exemplary `cacti` module instead.

Enhancing the agent through plugins

The reusable classes and defines give manifests that use your module much more expressive power. Installing and configuring Cacti now works concisely, and the manifest to do this becomes very readable and maintainable.

It's time to tap into the even more powerful aspect of modules—Puppet plugins. The different types of plugins are custom facts (which were discussed in *Chapter 3, A Peek Under the Hood – Facts, Types, and Providers*), parser functions, types, and providers. All these plugins are stored in the modules on the master and get synchronized to all the agents. The agent will not use the parser functions (they are available to users of `puppet apply` on the agent machine once they are synchronized, however), but facts and types do most of their work on the agent. Let's concentrate on types and providers for now—the other plugins will be discussed in dedicated sections later.

 This section can be considered optional. Many users will never touch the code for any type or provider—manifests give you all the flexibility you will ever need. On the other hand, if you are confident about your Ruby skills and would like to take advantage of them in your Puppet installations, read on to find the ways in which custom types and providers can help you.

While custom types are functional on both the master and the agent, the provider will do all its work on the agent side. While types also perform mainly through the agent, they have one effect on the master: they enable manifests to declare resources of the type. The code not only describes what properties and parameters exist, it can also include validation and transformation code for the respective values. This part is invoked by the agent. Some types even do the synchronization and queries themselves, although there is usually at least one provider that takes care of this.

In the previous section, you implemented a defined type that did all its synchronization by wrapping some exec resources. By installing binaries and scripts through Puppet, you can implement almost any kind of functionality this way and extend Puppet without ever writing one plugin. This does have some disadvantages, however:

- The output is cryptic in the ideal case and overwhelming in the case of errors
- Puppet shells out to at least one external process per resource; and in many cases, multiple forks are required

In short, you pay a price, both with the usability and the performance. Consider the cacti::device type. For each declared resource, Puppet will have to run an exec resource's unless query on each run (or onlyif when ensure=>absent is specified). This consists of one call to a PHP script (which can be expensive) as well as several core utilities that have to parse the output. On a Cacti server with dozens or hundreds of managed devices, these calls add up and make the agent spend a lot of time forking off and waiting for these child processes.

Consider a provider, on the other hand. It can implement an instances hook, which will create an internal list of configured Cacti devices once during initialization. This requires only one PHP call in total, and all the processing of the output can be done in the Ruby code directly inside the agent process. These savings alone will make each run much less expensive: resources that are already synchronized will incur no penalty, because no additional external commands need to be run.

Let's take a quick look at the agent output before we go ahead and implement a simple type/provider pair. This is the output of the cacti::device type when it creates a device:

```
Notice: /Stage[main]/Main/Node[agent]/Cacti::Device[Agent_VM_Debian_7]/
Exec[add-cacti-device-Agent_VM_Debian_7]/returns: executed successfully
```

The native types express such actions in a much cleaner manner, such as the output from a file resource:

```
Notice: /Stage[main]/Main/File[/usr/local/bin/cacti-search-graph]/ensure:
created
```

Replacing a defined type with a native type

The process of creating a custom type with a matching provider (or several providers) is not easy. Let's go through the following steps:

1. Naming your type.
2. Creating the resource type's interface.
3. Designing sensible parameter hooks.
4. Using resource names.
5. Adding a provider.
6. Declaring management commands.
7. Implementing the basic functionality.
8. Allowing the provider to prefetch existing resources.
9. Making the type robust during the provisioning.

Naming your type

The first important difference between native and defined types is the naming. There is no module namespacing for custom types like you get with the defined types, which are manifest-based. Native types from all installed modules mingle freely, if you will. They use plain names. It would, therefore, be unwise to call the native implementation of cacti::device just device—this will easily clash with whatever notion of *devices* another module might have. The obvious choice for naming your first type is cacti_device.

The type must be completely implemented in cacti/lib/puppet/type/cacti_device.rb. All hooks and calls will be enclosed in a Type.newtype block:

```
Puppet::Type.newtype(:cacti_device) do
  @doc = <<-EOD
    Manages Cacti devices.
    EOD
end
```

The documentation string in @doc should be considered mandatory, and it should be a bit more substantial than this example. Consider including one or more example resource declarations. Put all further code pieces between the EOD terminator and the final end.

Creating the resource type interface

First of all, the type should have the `ensure` property. Puppet types have a handy helper method that generates all the necessary type code for it through a simple invocation:

```
ensurable
```

With this method call in the body of the type, you add the typical `ensure` property, including all the hooks. Most properties and parameters require more code. Next up is the `ip` parameter:

```
require 'ipaddr'
newparam(:ip) do
  desc "The IP address of the device."
  isrequired
  validate do |value|
    begin
      IPAddr.new(value)
    rescue ArgumentError
      fail "'#{value}' is not a valid IP address"
    end
  end
  munge do |value|
    value.downcase
  end
end
```

> This should usually be an `ip` property instead, but the provider will rely on the Cacti CLI, which has no capability for changing the already configured devices. If the IP address was a property, such changes would be required in order to perform property-value synchronization.

As you can see, the IP address parameter code consists mostly of validation. Add the `require 'ipaddr'` line near the top of the file rather than in the `Type.newtype` block.

The parameter is now available for `cacti_device` resources, and the agent will even refuse to add devices whose IP addresses are not valid. This is helpful for users, because obvious typos in addresses will be detected early. Let's implement the next parameter before we look at the `munge` hook more closely.

Designing sensible parameter hooks

Moving right along to the `ping_method` parameter, it accepts only values from a limited set, so validation is easy:

```
newparam(:ping_method) do
  desc "How the device's reachability is determined.
    One of `tcp` (default), `udp` or `icmp`."
  validate do |value|
    [ :tcp, :udp, :icmp ].include?(value.downcase.to_sym)
  end
  munge do |value|
    value.downcase.to_sym
  end
  defaultto :tcp
end
```

Looking at the `munge` blocks carefully, you will notice that they aim at unifying input values. This is much less critical for parameters rather than properties, but if either of these parameters will be changed to a property in a future release of your Cacti module, it will not try and sync a `ping_method` of `tcp` to `TCP`, because the users prefer uppercase in their manifest. Both values just become `:tcp` through munging. For the IP address, invoking `downcase` has an effect only for IPv6.

> Beyond the scope of Puppet itself, the munging of a parameter's value is important as well. It allows Puppet to accept more convenient values than the subsystem being managed. For example, Cacti might not accept TCP as a value, but Puppet will, and it will do the right thing with it.

Using resource names

You need to take care of one final requirement: each Puppet resource type must declare a **name variable** or namevar, for short. This parameter will use the resource title from the manifest as its value if the parameter itself is not specified for the resource. For example, the `exec` type has the `command` parameter for its namevar. You can either put the executable command into the resource title or explicitly declare the parameter:

```
exec { '/bin/true': }
# same effect:
exec { 'some custom name': command => '/bin/true' }
```

To mark one of the existing parameters as the name variable, call the `isnamevar` method in that parameter's body. If a type has a parameter called `:name`, it automatically becomes the name variable. This is a safe default:

```
newparam(:name) do
  desc "The name of the device."
  #isnamevar # → commented because automatically assumed
end
```

Adding a provider

The type itself is ready for action, but it lacks a provider to do the actual work of inspecting the system and performing the synchronization. Let's build it step by step, just like the type. The name of the provider need not reflect the type it's for. Instead, it should contain a reference to the management approach it implements. Since your provider will rely on the Cacti CLI, name it `cli`. It's fine for multiple providers to share a name if they provide functionality to different types.

Create the skeleton structure in `cacti/lib/puppet/provider/cacti_device/cli.rb`:

```
Puppet::Type.type(:cacti_device).provide(
    :cli,
    :parent => Puppet::Provider
    ) do
end
```

Specifying `:parent => Puppet::Provider` is not necessary, actually. `Puppet::Provider` is the default base class for providers. If you write a couple of similar providers for a subsystem (each catering to a different resource type), all of which rely on the same toolchain, you might want to implement a base provider that becomes the parent for all sibling providers.

For now, let's concentrate on putting together a self-sufficient `cli` provider for the `cacti_device` type. First of all, declare the commands that you are going to need.

Declaring management commands

Providers use the `commands` method to conveniently bind executables to Ruby identifiers:

```
commands :php       => 'php'
commands :add_device => '/usr/share/cacti/cli/add_device.php'
commands :add_graphs => '/usr/share/cacti/cli/add_graphs.php'
commands :rm_device => '/usr/share/cacti/cli/remove_device.php'
```

You won't be invoking php directly. It's included here because declaring commands serves two purposes:

- You can conveniently call the commands through a generated method
- The provider will mark itself as valid only if all commands are found

So, if the php CLI command is not found in Puppet's search path, it will consider the provider to be dysfunctional. The user can determine this error condition quite quickly through Puppet's debug output.

Implementing the basic functionality

The basic functions of the provider can now be implemented in three instance methods. The names of these methods are not magic as such, but these are the methods that the default ensure property expects to be available (remember that you used the ensurable shortcut in the type code).

The first is the method that creates a resource if it does not exist yet. It must gather all the resource parameter's values and build an appropriate call to add_device.php:

```
def create
  args = []
  args << "--description=#{resource[:name]}"
  args << "--ip=#{resource[:ip]}"
  args << "--ping_method=#{resource[:ping_method]}"
  add_device(*args)
end
```

> Don't quote the parameter values as you would quote them on the command line. Puppet takes care of this for you. It also escapes any quotes that are in the arguments, so in this case, Cacti will receive any quotes to be included in the configuration. For example, this will lead to a wrong title:
>
> ```
> args << "--description='#{resource[:name]}'"
> ```

The provider must also be able to remove or destroy an entity:

```
def destroy
  rm_device("--device-id=#{@property_hash[:id]}")
end
```

The property_hash variable is an instance member of the provider. Each resource gets its specific provider instance. Read on to learn how it gets initialized to include the device's ID number.

Before we get to that, let's add the final provider method in order to implement the `ensure` property. This is a query method that the agent uses to determine whether a resource is already present:

```
def exists?
  self.class.instances.find do |provider|
    provider.name == resource[:name]
  end
end
```

The `ensure` property relies on the provider class method `instances` in order to get a list of `providers` for all entities on the system. It compares each of them with the `resource` attribute, which is the resource type instance for which this current provider instance is performing the work.

Allowing the provider to prefetch existing resources

The `instances` method is truly special—it implements the prefetching of system resources during the provider initialization. You have to add it to the provider yourself. Some subsystems are not suitable for the mass-fetching of all existing resources (such as the `file` type). These providers don't have an `instances` method:

```
def self.instances
  return @instances ||= add_graphs("--list-hosts").
    split("\n").
    drop(1).
    collect do |line|
      fields = line.split(/\t/, 4)
      Puppet.debug "prefetching cacti_device #{fields[3]} " +
                   "with ID #{fields[0]}"
      new(:ensure => :present,
          :name   => fields[3],
          :id     => fields[0])
    end
end
```

The `ensure` value of the provider instance reflects the current state. The method creates instances for resources that are found on the system, so for these, the value is always `present`. Also note that the result of the method is cached in the `@instances` class' member variable. This is important, because the `exists?` method calls `instances`, which can happen a lot.

Puppet requires another method to perform proper prefetching. The mass-fetching you implemented through `instances` supplies the agent with a list of provider instances that represent the entities found on the system. From the master, the agent received a list of type instances. However, Puppet has not yet built a relation between the resources (type instances) and providers. You need to add a `prefetch` method to the provider class in order to make this happen:

```
def self.prefetch(resources)
  instances.each do |provider|
    if res = resources[provider.name]
      res.provider = provider
    end
  end
end
```

The agent passes the `cacti_device` resources as a hash, with the resource title as the respective key. This makes lookups very simple (and quick).

This completes the `cli` provider for the `cacti_device` type. You can now replace your `cacti::device` resources with `cacti_device` instances and enjoy improved performance and cleaner agent output:

```
node 'agent' {
    include cacti
    cacti_device {
        'Puppet test agent (Debian 7)':
            ensure => present,
            ip => $ipaddress;
    }
}
```

Please note that unlike your defined type `cacti::device`, a native type will not assume a default value of `present` for its `ensure` property. Therefore, you have to specify it for any `cacti_device` resource. Otherwise, Puppet will only manage properties of resources that already exist and not care about whether the entity exists or not. In the particular case of `cacti_device`, this will never do anything, because there are no other properties (only parameters).

> You can refer to *Chapter 6, Leveraging the Full Toolset of the Language*, on how to use resource defaults to save you from the repetition of the `ensure => present` specification.

Making the type robust during provisioning

There is yet another small issue with the `cacti` module. It is self-sufficient and handles both the installation and configuration of Cacti. However, this means that during Puppet's first run, the `cacti` package and its CLI will not be available, and the agent will correctly determine that the `cli` provider is not yet suitable. Since it is the only provider for the `cacti_device` type, any resource of this type that is synchronized before the `cacti` package will fail.

In the case of the defined type `cacti::device`, you just added `require` metaparameters to the inner resources. To achieve the same end for native type instances, you can work with the **autorequire** feature. Just like files automatically depend on their containing directory, the Cacti resources should depend on the successful synchronization of the `cacti` package. Add the following block to the `cacti_device` type:

```
autorequire :package do
  catalog.resource(:package, 'cacti')
end
```

Enhancing Puppet's system knowledge through facts

When facts were introduced in *Chapter 3, A Peek Under the Hood – Facts, Types, and Providers*, you got a small tour of the process of creating your own custom facts. I hinted at modules at this point, and now, we can take a closer look at how fact code is deployed, using the example of the `Cacti` module. Let's focus on native Ruby facts—they are more portable than external facts. As the latter are easier to create, there is no need to discuss them in depth here.

 For details on external facts, you can refer to the online documentation on custom facts on the Puppet Labs site at `https://docs.puppetlabs.com/facter/2.1/custom_facts.html#external-facts`.

Facts are part of the Puppet plugins that a module can contain, just like the types and providers from the previous sections. They belong in the `lib/facter/` subtree.

For users of the `cacti` module, it might be helpful to learn which graph templates are available on a given Cacti server (once the graph management is implemented, that is). The complete list can be passed through a fact.

With Facter 2.x, you can handle the list as an array. If your module should retain compatibility with Facter 1.x, the fact value should be a string representation of the list — usually the comma-separated concatenation of all list values.

The following code in `cacti/lib/facter/cacti_graph_templates.rb` will do just this job:

```
Facter.add(:cacti_graph_templates) do
  setcode do
    cmd = '/usr/share/cacti/cli/add_graphs.php'
    Facter::Core::Execution.exec("#{cmd} --list-graph-templates").
      split("\n").
      drop(1).
      collect do |line|
        line.split(/\t/)[1]
      end
  end
end
```

The code will call the CLI script, skip its first line of output, and join the values from the second column of each remaining line in a list. Manifests can access this list through the global `$cacti_graph_templates` variable, just like any other fact.

Refining the interface of your module through custom functions

Functions can be of great help in order to keep your manifest clean and maintainable, and many tasks cannot even be implemented without resorting to a Ruby function. This is because the Puppet language is rather minimalistic. This is a virtue, actually, because the language is easy to learn and the code is usually quite readable.

Among the problems that cannot be solved without functions are data transformations such as the joining of arrays, extracting the defined keys from a hash, and similar operations. The most useful of these types of data structure methods are implemented in the `stdlib` module.

Another frequent use for custom functions is input validation. You can do this in the manifest itself, but it can be a frustrating exercise because of the limitations of the language. The resulting Puppet DSL code can be hard to read and maintain. The `stdlib` module comes with `validate_X` functions for many basic data types, such as `validate_bool`.

As with all plugins, the functions need not be specific to the module's domain, and they instantly become available for all manifests. Point in case is the `cacti` module that can use validation functions for the `cacti::device` parameters. Checking whether a string contains a valid IP address is not at all specific to Cacti. On the other hand, checking whether the `ping_method` is one of those that Cacti recognizes is not that generic.

To see how it works, let's just implement a function that does the job of the `validate` and `munge` hooks from the custom `cacti_device` type for the IP address parameter of `cacti::device`. This should fail the compilation if the address is invalid; otherwise, it should return the unified address value:

```
module Puppet::Parser::Functions
  require 'ipaddr'
  newfunction(:cacti_canonical_ip, :type => :rvalue) do |args|
    ip = args[0]
    begin
      IPAddr.new(ip)
    rescue ArgumentError
      raise "#{@resource.ref}: invalid IP address '#{ip}'"
    end
    ip.downcase
  end
end
```

In the exception message, `@resource.ref` is expanded to the textual reference of the offending type instance, such as `Cacti::Device[Edge Switch 03]`.

The following example illustrates the use of the function in the simple version of `cacti::device` without the `ensure` parameter:

```
define cacti::device($ip) {
    $cli = '/usr/share/cacti/cli'
    $c_ip = cacti_canonical_ip($ip)
    $options = "--description='$name' --ip='$c_ip'"
    exec {
        "add-cacti-device-$name":
            command => "$cli/add_device.php $options",
            require => Class[cacti],
    }
}
```

The manifest will then fail to compile if an IP address has (conveniently) transposed digits:

```
ip => '912.168.12.13'
```

IPv6 addresses will be converted to all lowercase letters.

Making your module portable across platforms

Sadly, our Cacti module is very specific to the Debian package. It expects to find the CLI at a certain place and the Apache configuration snippet at another. These locations are most likely specific to the Debian package. It will be useful for the module to work on Red Hat derivatives as well.

The first step is to get an overview of the differences by performing a manual installation. I chose to test this with a virtual machine running Fedora 18. The basic installation is identical to Debian, except using yum instead of apt-get, of course. Puppet will automatically do the right thing here. The puppet::install class also contains a CLI file, though. The Red Hat package installs the CLI in /var/lib/cacti/cli rather than /usr/share/cacti/cli.

If the module is supposed to support both platforms, the target location for the remove_device.php script is no longer fixed. Therefore, it's best to deploy the script from a central location in the module, while the target location on the agent system becomes a module parameter, if you will. Such values are customarily gathered in a params class:

```
# .../cacti/manifests/params.pp
class cacti::params {
    case $osfamily {
        'Debian': {
            $cli_path = '/usr/share/cacti/cli'
        }
        'RedHat': {
            $cli_path = '/var/lib/cacti/cli'
        }
        default: {
            fail "the cacti module does not yet support the $osfamily
platform"
        }
    }
}
```

It is best to fail the compilation for unsupported agent platforms. The users will have to remove the declaration of the cacti class from their module rather than have Puppet try untested installation steps that most likely cannot work (this might concern Gentoo or a BSD variant).

Classes that need to access the variable value must include the params class:

```
class cacti::install {
    include cacti::params
    file {
        'remove_device.php':
            ensure => 'file',
            path    =>
                "${cacti::params::cli_path}/remove_device.php",
            source =>
                'puppet:///modules/cacti/cli/remove_device.php',
            mode   => 755;
    }
}
```

Similar transformations will be required for the cacti::redirect class and the cacti::config class. Just add more variables to the params class. This is not limited to the manifests, either—facts and providers must behave in accordance with the agent platform as well.

You will often see that the params class is inherited rather than included:

```
class cacti($redirect = $cacti::params::redirect)
        inherits cacti::params
{
    # ...
}
```

This is done because an include statement in the class body won't allow the use of variable values from the params class as class parameter's default values, such as the $redirect parameter in this example.

The portability practices are often not required for your own custom modules. In the ideal case, you won't use them on more than one platform. The practice should be considered mandatory if you intend to share them on the Forge, though. For most of your Puppet needs, you will not want to write modules anyway but want to download existing solutions from the Forge instead.

Finding helpful Forge modules

Using the web interface at `http://forge.puppetlabs.com` is very straightforward. By filling in the search form with the name of the software, system, or service you need to manage, you will usually get a list of very fitting modules—often with just your search term as their name. In fact, for common terms, the number of available modules can be overwhelming.

You get immediate feedback about the maturity and popularity of each module. A module is being actively used and maintained if:

- It has a version number that indicates releases past 1.0.0 (or even 0.1.0)
- Its most recent release was not too long ago, perhaps less than half a year
- It has a significant number of downloads

All these numbers can vary a lot, though, depending on the number of features that the module implements and how widespread its subject is. Even more importantly, just because a particular module gets much attention and regular contributions, this does not have to mean that it is the best choice for your situation.

You are encouraged to evaluate less trafficked modules as well—you can unearth some hidden gems this way. The next section details some deeper indicators of quality for you to take into consideration.

If you cannot or don't want to spend too much time digging for the best module, you can also just refer to the sidebar with the **Puppet Supported** and **Puppet Approved** modules. All modules that are featured in these categories got a seal of quality from Puppet Labs.

Identifying modules' characteristics

When navigating to a module's details in the Forge, you are presented with its README file. An empty or very sparse documentation speaks of little care taken by the module author. A sample manifest in the README file is often a good starting point in order to put a module to work quickly.

If you are looking for a module that will enhance your agents through additional types and providers, look for the **Types** tab on the module details page. For some modules, the type documentation won't be imported on the Forge, though. It's safer to click on the **Project URL** link near the top of the module description. This usually leads to GitHub. Here, you can conveniently browse not only the plugins in the `lib/` subtree, but also get a feel of how the module's manifests are structured.

Another sign of a carefully maintained module are unit tests. These are found in the spec/ subtree. This tree does exist for most Forge modules. It tends to be devoid of actual tests, though. There can be test code files for all classes and defined types that are part of the module's manifest—these are typically in the spec/classes/ and spec/defines/ subdirectories, respectively. For plugins, there will ideally be unit tests in spec/unit/ and spec/functions/.

Some README files of modules contain a small greenish tag saying **build passing**. This can turn red on occasion, stating **build failing**. These modules use the Travis CI through GitHub, so they are likely to have at least a few unit tests.

Summary

All the development in Puppet should be done in modules, and each such module should serve as specific a purpose as possible. Most modules comprise only manifests. This suffices to provide for very effective and readable node manifests that clearly and concisely express their intent by including aptly named classes and instantiating defined types.

Modules can also contain Puppet plugins in the form of types and providers, parser functions, or facts. All of these are usually Ruby code. External facts can be written in any language, though. Writing your own types and providers is not required, but it can boost your performance and management flexibility.

It is not necessary to write all your modules yourself—on the contrary, it's advisable to rely on open source modules from the Puppet Forge as much as possible. The Puppet Forge is an ever-growing collection of helpful code for virtually all systems and software that Puppet can manage. In particular, the modules that are curated by Puppet Labs are usually of very high quality. As with any open source software, you are more than welcome to add any missing requirements to the modules yourself.

After this broad view on Puppet's larger building blocks, the next chapter narrows the scope a little. Now that you have the tools to structure and compose a manifest code base, you will learn some refined techniques in order to elegantly solve some distinct problems with Puppet.

6
Leveraging the Full Toolset of the Language

After our in-depth discussions on both the manifest structure elements (class and define) and encompassing structure (modules), you are in a great position to write manifests for all of your agents. Make sure that you get Forge modules that will do your work for you. Then, go ahead and add site-specific modules that supply composite classes for the node blocks to be used (rather, included).

These concepts are quite a bit to take in. It's now time to decelerate a bit, lean back, and tackle simpler code structures and ideas. You are about to learn some techniques that you are not going to need every day. They can make difficult scenarios much easier, though. So, it might be a good idea to come back to this chapter again after you have spent some time in the field. You might find that some of your designs can be simplified with these tools.

Specifically, these are the techniques that will be presented:

- Templating dynamic configuration files
- Creating virtual resources
- Exporting resources to other agents
- Overriding resource parameters
- Making classes more flexible through inheritance
- Saving redundancy using resource defaults
- Avoiding antipatterns

Templating dynamic configuration files

In the introduction, I stated that the techniques that you are now learning are not frequently required. That was true except for this one topic. Templates are actually a cornerstone of configuration management with Puppet.

Templates are an alternative way to manage configuration files or any files, really. You have synchronized files from the master to an agent that handled some Apache configuration settings. These are not templates, technically. They are merely static files that have been prepared and are ready for carbon copying.

These static files suffice in many situations, but sometimes, you will want the master to manage very specific configuration values for each agent. These values can be quite individual. For example, an Apache server usually requires a `MaxClients` setting. Appropriate values depend on many aspects, including hardware specifications and characteristics of the web application that is being run. It would be impractical to prepare all possible choices as distinct files in the module.

Learning the template syntax

Templates make short work of such scenarios. If you are familiar with ERB templates already, you can safely skip to the next section. If you know your way around PHP or JSP, you will quickly get the hang of ERB—it's basically the same but with Ruby inside the code tags. The following template will produce `Hello, world!` three times:

```
<% ( 1 .. 3 ).each do %>
Hello, world!
<% end %>
```

This template will also produce lots of empty lines, because the text between the `<%` and `%>` tags gets removed from the output but the final line breaks do not. To make the ERB engine do just that, change the closing tag to `-%>`:

```
<% ( 1 .. 3 ).each do -%>
Hello, world!
<% end -%>
```

This example is not very helpful for configuration files, of course. To include dynamic values in the output, enclose Ruby expressions in a `<%= tag` pair:

```
<% ( 1 .. 3 ).each do |index| -%>
Hello, world #<%= index %> !
<% end -%>
```

Now, the iterator value is part of each line of the output. You can also use member variables that are prefixed with @.

These variables are populated with the values from the Puppet manifest variables:

```
<IfModule mpm_worker_module>
  ServerLimit          <%= @apache_server_limit %>
  StartServers         <%= @apache_start_servers %>
  MaxClients           <%= @apache_max_clients %>
</IfModule>
<% @apache_ports.each do |port| -%>
Listen <%= port %>
NameVirtualHost *:<%= port %>
<% end -%>
```

Variables that are used in a template must be defined in the same scope or scopes from which the template is used. The next section explains how this works.

In Puppet 3.x, variable values are mostly strings, arrays, or hashes. To write efficient templates, it is helpful to occasionally glance at the methods available for the respective Ruby classes. In Puppet 4, variables have more diverse values.

Using templates in practice

Templates have their own place in modules. You can place them freely in the templates/ subtree of the module. The template function locates them using a simple rule:

```
template('cacti/apache/cacti.conf.erb')
```

This expression evaluates the content of the template found in modules/cacti/templates/apache/cacti.conf.erb. The first path element (without a leading slash) is the module name. The rest of the path gets translated to the templates/ tree in the module. The function is commonly used to generate the value of a file resource's content property:

```
file { '/etc/apache2/conf.d/cacti.conf':
    content => template('cacti/apache/cacti.conf.erb'),
}
```

Many templates expect some variables to be defined in their scope. The easiest way to make sure that this happens is to wrap the respective file resource in a parameterized container. Files that are **singletons** with a well-known name such as /etc/ssh/sshd_config should be managed through a parameterized class. Configuration items that can inhabit multiple files such as /etc/logrotate.d/* or /etc/apache2/conf.d/* are well suited to be wrapped in defined types:

```
define logrotate::conf($pattern,$max_days=7,$options=[]) {
    file { "/etc/logrotate.d/$name":
```

```
        mode    => '644',
        content => template('logrotate/config-snippet.erb')
    }
}
```

In the preceding example, the template will use the parameters as `@pattern`, `@max_days`, and `@options`, respectively.

For a quick and dirty string transformation of your data, you can also use the `inline_template` function in your manifest. This is often found on the right-hand side of a variable assignment:

```
$comma_seperated_list = inline_template('<%= @my_array * "," %>')
```

This example assumes that the `$my_array` Puppet variable does hold an array value.

Avoiding performance bottlenecks from templates

When using templates, both through the `template` and the `inline_template` functions, be aware that each invocation implies a performance penalty for your Puppet master. During the compilation of the catalog, Puppet must initialize the ERB engine for any template it encounters. The ERB evaluation happens in an individual environment that is derived from the respective scope of the `template` function invocation.

It is, therefore, not even important how complex your templates are. If your manifest requires frequent expansion of a very short template, it generates an enormous overhead for each initialization. Especially in the case of an easy `inline_template` function such as the one mentioned previously, it can be worthwhile to invest some more effort in creating a `parser function` instead, as seen in *Chapter 5, Extending Your Puppet Infrastructure with Modules*. A function can perform variable value transformation without incurring the cumulative penalty.

On the bright side, using templates is quite economic for the agent, who receives the whole textual file content right inside the catalog. There is no need to make an additional call to the master and retrieve file metadata. On a high-latency network, this can be a noticeable saving.

There is no silver bullet here. Don't let the performance implications deter you from turning specific configuration files into templates. Template-based solutions will often make your module more maintainable, which will usually offset performance implications—hardware is constantly getting cheaper, after all. Just don't be wasteful with frequent (and simple) expansions.

Creating virtual resources

The next technique that we are going to discuss helps you solve conflicts in your manifests and build some elegant solutions in special situations.

Remember the uniqueness constraint that was introduced in *Chapter 1, Writing Your First Manifests*. Any resource must be declared at most once in a manifest. There cannot be two classes or defined type instances that declare the same `file`, `package`, or any other type of resource. Each resource must have a unique type/name combination. This applies to instances of defined types as well as native resources.

This can pose issues when multiple modules need a common resource, such as an installed package, or perhaps even independent settings in the same configuration file. A component class for such resources, as introduced in *Chapter 4, Modularizing Manifests with Classes and Defined Types*, will resolve basic conflicts of this kind. It can be included an arbitrary number of times in the same manifest.

This can be impractical when the number of shared resources is fairly large. Imagine that you find yourself in a situation where a large number of different Puppet nodes require software from a significant set of `yum` repositories. Puppet will happily manage the repository configuration on the agents through its `yumrepo` type. However, you don't actually want all these repositories configured on every last machine—they do incur maintenance overhead after all. It would, instead, be desirable for each node to automatically receive the configuration for all repositories it requires for its packages but not more.

When solving this using component classes, you would wrap each repository in a distinct class. The class names should closely resemble (and most likely contain) the name of the respective repositories:

```
class yumrepos::team_ninja_stable {
    yumrepo {
        'team_ninja_stable':
            ensure => present,
            ...
    }
}
```

Package resources that rely on one or more such repositories will need to be accompanied by appropriate `include` statements:

```
include yumrepos::team_ninja_stable
include yumrepos::team_wizard_experimental
package {
    'doombunnies':
```

```
        ensure => installed,
        require => Class[
            'yumrepos::team_ninja_stable',
            'yumrepos::team_wizard_experimental'
        ],
    }
```

This is possible, but it is obviously less than ideal. Puppet does offer an alternative way to avoid duplicate resource declarations in the form of virtual resources. It allows you to add a resource declaration to your manifest without adding the resource to the actual catalog. The virtual resource must be **realized** or **collected** for this purpose. Just like class inclusion, this realization of virtual resources can happen arbitrarily in the same manifest.

Our previous example can, therefore, use a simpler structure with just one class to declare all the yum repositories as virtual resources:

```
class yumrepos::all {
    @yumrepo {
        'team_ninja_stable':
            ensure => present,
            ...;
        'team_wizard_experimental': ...
        ...
    }
}
```

The @ prefix marks the yumrepo resources as virtual. This class can be safely included by all nodes. It will not affect the catalog until the resources are realized:

```
realize(Yumrepo['team_ninja_stable'])
realize(Yumrepo['team_wizard_experimental'])
package {
    'doombunnies':
        ensure => installed,
        require => Yumrepo[
            'team_ninja_stable', 'team_wizard_experimental'
        ],
}
```

The realize function converts the referenced virtual resources to real ones, which get added to the catalog. Granted, this is not much better than the previous code that relied on the component classes. The virtual resources do make the intent clearer, at least. Realizing them is less ambiguous than some include statements—a class can contain many resources and even more include statements.

To really improve the situation, you can introduce a defined type that can realize the repositories directly:

```
define curated::package($ensure,$repositories=[]) {
    if $repositories != [] and $ensure != 'absent' {
        realize(Yumrepo[$repositories])
    }
    package { $name: ensure => $ensure }
}
```

You can then just pass the names of yumrepo resources for realization:

```
curated::package {
    'doombunnies':
        ensure => 'installed',
        repositories => [
            'team_ninja_stable',
            'team_wizard_experimental',
        ],
}
```

Better yet, you can most likely prepare a hash, globally or in the scope of curated::package, to create the most common resolutions:

```
$default_repos = {
    'doombunnies' => [
        'team_ninja_stable',
        'team_wizard_experimental',
    ],
    ...
}
```

The curated::package can then look packages up if no explicit repository names are passed. Use the has_key function from the puppetlabs-stdlib module to make the lookup safer:

```
if $repositories != [] {
    realize(Yumrepo[$repositories])
}
elsif has_key($default_repos,$name) {
    $repolist = $default_repos[$name]
    realize(Yumrepo[$repolist])
}
```

This `define` structure is actually possible with component classes as well. The class names can be passed as a parameter or from a central data structure. The `include` function will accept variable values for class names.

Realizing resources more flexibly using collectors

Instead of invoking the `realize` function, you can also rely on a different syntactic construct, which is the `collector`:

```
Yumrepo<| title == 'team_ninja_stable' |>
```

This is more flexible than the function call at the cost of a slight performance penalty. It can be used as a reference to the realized resource(s) in certain contexts. For example, you can add ordering constraints with the chaining operator:

```
Yumrepo<| title == 'team_ninja_stable' |> -> Class['...']
```

It is even possible to change values of resource attributes during collection. There is a whole section dedicated to such overrides later in this chapter.

As the collector is based on an expression, you can conveniently realize a whole range of resources. This can be quite dynamic—sometimes, you will create virtual resources that are already being realized by a rather indiscriminate collector. Let's look at a common example:

```
User<| |>
```

With no expression, the collection encompasses all virtual resources of the given type. This allows you to collect them all, without worrying about their concrete titles or attributes. This might seem redundant, because then it makes no sense to declare the resources as virtual in the first place. However, keep in mind that the collector might appear in some select manifests only, while the virtual resources can be safely added to all your nodes.

To be a little more selective, it can be useful to group virtual resources based on their **tags**. We haven't discussed tags yet. Each resource is tagged with several identifiers. Each tag is just a simple string. You can tag a resource manually by defining the `tag` metaparameter:

```
file { '/etc/sysctl.conf': tag => 'security' }
```

The named tag is added to the resource. Puppet implicitly tags all resources with the name of the declaring class, the containing module, and a range of other useful meta information. For example, if your user module divides the `user` resources in classes such as `administrators`, `developers`, `qa`, and other roles, you can make certain nodes or classes select all users of a given role with a collection based on the class name tag:

```
User<| tag == 'developers' |>
```

Note that the tags actually form an array. The `==` comparison will look for the presence of the `developers` element in the `tag` array in this context. Have a look at another example to make this more clear:

```
@user {
    'felix':
        ensure => present,
        groups => [ 'power', 'sys' ],
}
User<| groups == 'sys' |>
```

This way, you can collect all users who are members of the `sys` group.

If you prefer function calls over the more cryptic collector syntax, you can keep using the `realize` function alongside collectors. This works without issues. Remember that each resource can be realized multiple times, even in both ways, simultaneously.

If you are wondering, the manifest for a given agent can only realize virtual resources that are declared inside this same agent's manifest. Virtual resources do not leak into other manifests. Consequently, there can be no deliberate transfer of resources from one manifest to another, either. However, there is yet another concept that allows such an exchange; this is described in the next section.

Exporting resources to other agents

Puppet is commonly used to configure whole clusters of servers or HPC workers. Any configuration management system makes this task very efficient in comparison to manual care. Manifests can be shared between similar nodes. Configuration items that require individual customization per node are modeled individually. The whole process is very natural and direct.

On the other hand, there are certain configuration tasks that do not lend themselves well to the paradigm of the central definition of all states. For example, a cluster setup might include the sharing of a generated key or registering IP addresses of peer nodes as they become available. An automatic setup should include an exchange of such shared information. Puppet can help out with this as well.

This is a very good fit. It saves a metalayer, because you don't need to implement the setup of an information exchange system in Puppet. The sharing is secure, relying on Puppet's authentication and encryption infrastructure. There is logging and central control over the deployment of the shared configuration. Puppet retains its role as the central source for all system details. It serves as a hub for a secure exchange of information.

Exporting and importing resources

Puppet approaches the problem of sharing configuration information among multiple agent nodes by way of exported resources. The concept is simple. The manifest of node A can contain one or more resources that are purely virtual and not for realization in the manifest of this node A. Other nodes, such as B and C, can import some or all of these resources. Then, the resources become part of the catalogs of these remote nodes.

The syntax to import and export resources is very similar to that of virtual resources. An exported resource is declared by prepending the resource type name with two @ characters:

```
@@file {
    'my-app-psk':
        path    => '/etc/my-app/psk',
        content => 'nwNFgzsn9n3sDfnFANfoinaAEF',
        tag     => 'cluster02',
}
```

The importing manifests collect these resources using an expression, which is again similar to the collection of virtual resources but with double-angled brackets, < and >:

```
File<<| tag == 'cluster02' |>>
```

Tags are a very common way to take fine-grained control over the distribution of such exported resources.

Configuring the master to store exported resources

The best way to enable support for exported resources is PuppetDB. It is a domain-specific database implementation that stores different kinds of data that the Puppet master deals with during regular operation. This includes catalog requests from agents (including their valuable facts), reports from catalog applications, and exported resources.

Chapter 2, The Master and Its Agents, detailed a manual installation of the master. Let's add the PuppetDB with more style—through Puppet! On the Forge, you will find a convenient module that will make this easy:

```
puppet module install puppetlabs-puppetdb
```

On the master node, the setup now becomes a one-line invocation:

```
puppet apply -e 'include puppetdb, puppetdb::master::config'
```

As our test master uses a nonstandard SSL certificate that is named `master.example.net` (instead of its FQDN), it must be configured for `puppetdb` as well:

```
include puppetdb
class {
    'puppetdb::master::config':
        puppetdb_server => 'master.example.net'
}
```

The ensuing catalog run is quite impressive. Puppet installs the PostgreSQL backend, the Jetty server, and the actual PuppetDB package; configures everything and starts the services up—all in one go. After applying this short manifest, you have added a complex piece of infrastructure to your Puppet setup. You can now use exported resources for a variety of helpful tasks.

Exporting SSH host keys

For home-grown interactions between clustered machines, SSH can be an invaluable tool. File transfer and remote execution of arbitrary commands is easily possible, thanks to the ubiquitous `sshd` service. For security reasons, each host generates a unique key in order to identify itself. Of course, such public key authentication systems can only really work with a trust network or the presharing of the public keys. Puppet can do the latter quite nicely:

```
@@sshkey {
    $fqdn:
        host_aliases => $hostname,
        key          => $sshecdsakey,
        tag          => 'san-nyc'
}
```

Interested nodes collect keys with the known pattern:

```
Sshkey<<| tag == 'san-nyc' |>>
```

Now, SSH servers can be authenticated through the respective keys that Puppet safely stores in its database. As always, the Puppet master is the fulcrum of security.

Managing hosts files locally

Many sites can rely a local DNS infrastructure. Resolving names to local IP addresses is easy with such setups. However, small networks or sites that consist of many independent clusters with little shared infrastructure will have to rely on names in /etc/hosts instead.

You can maintain a central hosts file per network cell, or you can make Puppet maintain each entry in each hosts file separately. The latter approach has some advantages:

- Changes are automatically distributed through the Puppet agent network
- Puppet copes with unmanaged lines in the hosts files

A manually maintained registry is prone to be outdated every once in a while. It will also obliterate local additions in any hosts files on the agent machines.

The manifest implementation is very similar to the PKI from the previous section:

```
@@host {
    $fqdn:
        ip            => $ipaddress,
        host_aliases => [ $hostname ],
        tag           => 'nyc-site',
}
```

This is the same principle, only now each node exports its $ipaddress fact value alongside its name and not a public key. The import also works the same way:

```
Host<<| tag == 'nyc-site' |>>
```

Automating custom configuration items

Do you remember the Cacti module that you created during the previous chapter? It makes it very simple to configure all monitored devices in the manifest of the Cacti server. However, as this is possible, wouldn't it be even better if each node in your network was registered automatically with Cacti? It's simple—make the devices export their respective cacti_device resources for the server to collect:

```
@@cacti_device {
    $fqdn:
        ensure => present,
        ip  => $ipaddress,
        tag => 'nyc-site',
}
```

The Cacti server, apart from including the `cacti` class, just needs to collect the devices now:

```
Cacti_device<<| tag == 'nyc-site' |>>
```

If one Cacti server handles all your machines, you can just omit the `tag` comparison:

```
Cacti_device<<| |>>
```

Once the module supports other Cacti resources, you can handle them in the same way. Let's look at an example from another popular monitoring solution.

Simplifying the Nagios configuration

Puppet comes with support to manage the complete configuration of Nagios (and compatible versions of Icinga). Each configuration section can be represented by a distinct Puppet resource with types such as `nagios_host` or `nagios_service`.

 There is an endeavor to remove this support from core Puppet. This does not mean that support will be discontinued, however. It will just move to yet another excellent Puppet module.

Each of your machines can export their individual `nagios_host` resources alongside their `host` and `cacti_device` resources. However, thanks to the diverse Nagios support, you can do even better.

Assuming that you have a module or class to wrap SSH handling (you are using a Forge module for the actual management, of course), you can handle monitoring from inside your own SSH server class. By adding the export to this class, you make sure that nodes that include the class (and only these nodes) will also get monitoring:

```
class site::ssh {
    # ...actual SSH management...
    @@nagios_service {
        "${fqdn}-ssh":
            use             => 'ssh_template',
            host_name       => $fqdn,
    }
}
```

You probably know the drill by now, but let's repeat the mantra once more:

```
Nagios_service<<| |>>
```

With this collection, the Nagios host configures itself with all services that the agent manifests create.

 For large Nagios configurations, you might want to consider reimplementing the Nagios types yourself using simple defines that build the configuration from templates. The native types can be slower than the `file` resources in this case, because they have to parse the whole Nagios configuration on each run. The `file` resources can be much cheaper, as they rely on content-agnostic checksums.

Maintaining your central firewall

Speaking of useful features that are not part of core Puppet, you can manage the rules of your `iptables` firewall, of course. You need the `puppetlabs-firewall` module to make the appropriate types available. Then, each machine can (among other useful things) export its own required port forwarding to the firewall machines:

```
@@firewall {
    "150 forward port 443 to $hostname":
        proto  => 'tcp',
        dport  => '443',
        destination => $public_ip_address,
        jump   => 'DNAT',
        todest => $ipaddress,
        tag    => 'segment03',
}
```

 The `$public_ip_address` value is not a Facter fact, of course. Your node will have to be configured with the appropriate information. You can refer to the next chapter for a good way to do this.

The title of a firewall rule resource conventionally begins with a three-digit index for ordering purposes. The firewall machines collect all these rules naturally:

```
Firewall<<| tag == 'segment03' |>>
```

As you can see, the possibilities for modeling distributed systems through exported Puppet resources are manifold. The simple pattern that we've iterated for several resource types suffices for a wide range of use cases. Combined with defined resource types, it allows you to flexibly enable your manifests to work together in order to form complex cluster setups with relatively little effort. The larger your clusters, the more work Puppet lifts from you through exports and collections.

Overriding resource parameters

Both exported and virtual resources are declared once and are then collected in different contexts. The syntax is very similar, as are the concepts.

Sometimes, a central definition of a resource cannot be safely realized on all of your nodes, though; for example, consider the set of all your user resources. You will most likely wish to manage the user ID that is assigned to each account in order to make them consistent across your networks.

 This is often solved through LDAP or similar directories, but that is not possible for some sites.

Even if all accounts on almost all machines will be able to use their designated ID, there are likely to be some exceptions. On a few older machines, some IDs are probably being used for other purposes already, which cannot be changed easily. On such machines, creating users with these IDs will fail.

 The accounts can be created if duplicate IDs are allowed, but that is not a solution to this problem—duplicates are usually not desirable.

Fortunately, Puppet has a convenient way to express such exceptions. To give the felix user the nonstandard UID 2066, realize the resource with an attribute value specification:

```
User<| title == 'felix' |> {
    uid => '2066'
}
```

You can pass any property, parameter, or metaparameter that applies to the resource type in question. A value that you specify this way is final and cannot be overridden again.

This language feature is more powerful than the preceding example lets on. This is because the override is not limited to virtual and exported resources. You can override any resource from anywhere in your manifest. This allows for some remarkable constructs and shortcuts.

Consider, for example, the Cacti module that you created during the previous chapter. It declares a `package` resource in order to make sure that the software is installed. To that end, it specifies `ensure => installed`. If any user of your module needs Puppet to keep their packages up to date, this is not adequate though. The clean solution for this case is to add some parameters to the module's classes, which allow the user to choose the `ensure` property value for the package and other resources. However, this is not really practical. Complex modules can manage hundreds of properties, and exposing them all through parameters would form a horribly confusing interface.

The override syntax can provide a simple and elegant workaround here. The manifest that achieves the desired result is very straightforward:

```
include cacti
Package<| title == 'cacti' |> { ensure => 'latest' }
```

For all its simplicity, this manifest will be hard to decipher for collaborators who are not familiar with the collector/override syntax. This is not the only problem with overrides. You cannot override the same attribute multiple times. This is actually a good thing, because any rules that resolve such conflicting overrides make it extremely difficult to predict the actual semantics of a manifest that contains multiple overrides of this kind.

Relying on this override syntax too much will make your manifests prone to conflicts. Combining the wrong classes will make the compiler stop creating the catalog. Even if you manage to avoid all conflicts, the manifests will become rather chaotic. It can be difficult to locate all active overrides for a given node. The resulting behavior of any class or define becomes hard to predict.

All things considered, it's safest to use overrides very sparingly. The next section introduces a safer way to override parameters of some resources.

Making classes more flexible through inheritance

When you walked through the basic implementation of the Cacti module in the previous chapter, you probably noticed that the class is the backbone of any manifest. You add classes to your manifests for almost any new feature that you want to support. The class concept is pervasive and central to the majority of manifest designs. There is no alternative to relying on classes in the manifest development.

For all this, the class might lack some flexibility. A class will either just behave in a fixed way, or it will accept parameters for (practically unlimited) customization. The limitations of class parameterization have been discussed in *Chapter 4, Modularizing Manifests with Classes and Defined Types*. For component type classes that need to be available for inclusion from several (perhaps lots of) modules, parameters are usually out of the question.

Understanding class inheritance in Puppet

The Puppet DSL provides a compromise in the form of subclasses. When dealing with this topic, it is important to understand that inheritance in Puppet is a very different concept than its counterpart in object-oriented programming. There are some parallels: a Puppet subclass has access to its parent's variables, it implements the same basic semantics, and does some very specific additions or alterations. This is where the commonalities end for all practical intents and purposes. There is no common interface that all siblings present. There is no such thing as abstract base classes or methods. You never need to choose among alternative subclasses.

Making a class inherit another class mainly allows you to use one powerful construct—a localized resource override. The inheriting class can override any resource that was declared in any ancestor class:

```
class cacti::install {
    package { 'cacti': ensure => 'present' }
}
class cacti::install::update inherits cacti::install {
    Package['cacti'] { ensure => 'latest' }
}
```

Any node can opt to include the cacti::install::update class in addition to the cacti::install class. The override will take effect then. As usual, it does not matter how many include statements for either class appear in the manifest.

The override in the subclass uses the plain resource reference instead of the collector syntax that you discovered in the previous section. Overriding this way has some advantages. It is centralized in a class, so you avoid some possible conflicts.

Let's consider a different example in order to explain the significance. To manage your SSH infrastructure, you can create an SSH module, the ssh::config class will deploy your standard configuration from a template. It is implicitly included by most of your nodes. You also create some modules that manage solutions that rely on ssh and scp to pass information among machines. These modules should include the SSH classes as well, which, consequently, cannot be parameterized safely.

Some nodes need some customization, though. Assume that there are specific machines that should allow logging in with the root account directly:

```
class ssh::config {
    ssh::sshd_config_file {
        '/etc/ssh/sshd_config':
            listen => '0.0.0.0',
            keytypes => [ 'rsa', 'ecdsa' ],
    }
}
class ssh::config::allow_root inherits ssh::config {
    Ssh::Sshd_config_file['/etc/ssh/sshd_config'] {
        allow_root_login => true
    }
}
```

Not only can the whole ssh class (and by inclusion, the ssh::config class) be included as often as required, but you can also allow root login wherever appropriate by adding an include statement for the subclass:

```
include ssh::config::allow_root
```

This is an advantage over directly overriding the ssh::sshd_config_file resource through the collector syntax. If such an override appears in multiple modules, it renders them incompatible, because the overrides conflict with one another. Collector overrides form a conflict even if they try to assign the same attribute values.

There are limits to what you can do with subclasses as well. While it is not a problem for several sibling classes to override the same resource attribute, such classes cannot be included in the same manifest:

```
class ssh::config::allow_passwords inherits ssh::config {
    Ssh::Sshd_config_file['/etc/ssh/sshd_config'] {
        allow_root_login => false, # vs. dictionary attacks!
        allow_passwords  => true,
    }
}
```

The allow_passwords subclass obviously does not mix with the allow_root class. Trying to include both will result in a compiler error.

Naming an inheriting class

It bears mentioning that overrides through class inheritance are not really part of the community's best practices. It is not generally frowned upon, but it's a somewhat obscure feature. Many users have been known to avoid it in order to save their manifests from the additional complexity of yet another structural concept.

As such, there are no guidelines for naming subclasses. Gathering sibling classes in a pseudo-namespace under the parent class (such as the previous SSH example) is not a bad idea. It allows you to express the intent of the subclass clearly, and the name structure provides a clear hint at the inheritance relationship.

Making parameters safer through inheritance

This section's title might be misleading. Parameters and inheritance don't mix very well. A class that accepts parameters cannot be inherited. However, there is no rule that exempts subclasses from being parameterized. This allows for designs where the base class is included ubiquitously and arbitrarily, but customization through parameters is still a possibility:

```
class ssh::config::custom($listen = '0.0.0.0',
                          $allow_root_login = false,
                          $allow_passwords = false,
                          …) inherits ssh::config
{
    Ssh::Sshd_config_file['/etc/ssh/sshd_config'] {
        listen           => $listen,
        allow_root_login => $allow_root_login,
        allow_passwords  => $allow_passwords,
        …
    }
}
```

With this subclass, a node manifest can customize the SSH configuration in one declaration:

```
class {
    'ssh::config::custom':
        listen           => $ipaddress,
        allow_passwords  => true,
        allow_root_login => true,
}
```

This must be avoided in modules because the usual limitations of parameterized classes apply. Again, the virtue of this approach is that the base `ssh::config` class can be safely included from any module in your code base.

Saving redundancy using resource defaults

The final language construct that this chapter introduces can save you quite some typing, or rather, it saves you from copying and pasting. Writing a long, repetitive manifest is not what costs you lots of time, of course. However, a briefer manifest is often more readable, and hence, more maintainable. You achieve this by defining resource defaults—attribute values that are used for resources that don't choose their own:

```
Mysql_grant {
    ensure     => 'present',
    options    => ['GRANT'],
    privileges => ['ALL'],
    tables     => '*.*',
}
mysql_grant {
    'root':
        user  => 'root@localhost';
    'apache':
        user  => 'apache@10.0.1.%',
        tables => 'application.*';
    'wordpress':
        user  => 'wordpress@10.0.5.1',
        tables => 'wordpress.*';
    'backup':
        user  => 'backup@localhost',
        privileges => [ 'SELECT', 'LOCK TABLE' ];
}
```

By default, each grant should be present, apply to all databases, and comprise all privileges. This allows you to define each actual `mysql_grant` resource quite sparsely. Otherwise, you will have to specify the `privileges` property for all resources. The `ensure` and `options` attributes will be especially repetitive, because they are identical for all grants in this example.

 The `mysql_grant` resource type is not available in core Puppet. It's part of the `puppetlabs-mysql` module on the Forge.

Despite the convenience that this approach offers, it should not be used at each apparent opportunity. It has some downsides that you should keep in mind:

- The defaults can be surprising if they apply to resources that are declared at a lexical distance from the defaults' definition (such as several screens further down the manifest file)
- The defaults transcend the inclusion of classes and instantiation of defines

These two aspects form a dangerous combination. Defaults from a composite class can affect very distant parts of a manifest:

```
class webserver {
    include apache, nginx, firewall, logging_client
    File { owner => 'www-data' }
    file {
        ...
    }
}
```

Files declared in the `webserver` class should obviously belong to a default user. However, this default is in effect recursively in the included classes as well. The `owner` attribute is a property. A resource that defines no value for it just ignores its current state. A value that is specified in the manifest will be enforced by the agent. Often, you do not care about the owner of a managed file:

```
file { '/etc/motd': content => '...' }
```

However, because of the default `owner` attribute, Puppet will now mandate that this file belongs to `www-data`. To avoid this, you will have to unset the default by overwriting it with `undef`, which is Puppet's analog to the `nil` value:

```
File { owner => undef }
```

This can also be done in individual resources:

```
file { '/etc/motd': content => '...', owner => undef }
```

However, doing this constantly is hardly feasible. The latter option is especially unattractive, because it leads to more complexity in the manifest code instead of simplifying it. After all, not defining a default `owner` attribute will be the cleaner way here.

The semantics that make defaults take effect in so many manifest areas is known as **dynamic scoping**. It used to apply to variable values as well and is generally considered harmful. One of the most decisive changes in Puppet 3.0 was the removal of dynamic variable scoping, in fact. Resource defaults still use it, but it is expected that this will change in a future release as well.

Resource defaults should be used with consideration and care. For some properties such as file mode, owner, and group, they should usually be avoided.

Avoiding antipatterns

Speaking of things to avoid, there is a language feature that I will only address in order to advise great caution. Puppet comes with a function called defined that allows you to query the compiler about resources that have been declared in the manifest:

```
if defined(File['/etc/motd']) {
    notify { 'This machine has a MotD': }
}
```

The problem with the concept is that it cannot ever be reliable. Even if the resource appears in the manifest, the compiler might encounter it later than the if condition. This is potentially very problematic, because some modules will try to make themselves portable through this construct:

```
if ! defined(Package['apache2']) {
    package {
        'apache2':
            ensure => 'installed'
    }
}
```

The module author supposes that this resource definition will be skipped if the manifest declares Package['apache2'] somewhere else. As explained, this method will only be effective if the block is evaluated late enough during the compiler run. The conflict can still occur if the compiler encounters the other declaration *after* this one.

The manifest's behavior becomes outright unpredictable if a manifest contains multiple occurrences of the same query:

```
class cacti {
    if ! defined(Package['apache2']) {
```

```
        package { 'apache2': ensure => 'present' }
    }
}
class postfixadmin {
    if !defined(Package['apache2'] {
        package { 'apache2': ensure => 'latest' }
    }
}
```

The first block that is seen wins. This can even shift if unrelated parts of the manifest are restructured. You cannot predict whether a given manifest will use `ensure => latest` for the `apache2` package or just use `installed`. The results become even more bizarre if such a block wants a resource removed through `ensure => absent`, while the other does not.

The `defined` function has long been considered harmful, but there is no adequate alternative yet. The `ensure_resource` function from the `stdlib` module tries to make the scenario less problematic:

```
ensure_resource('package', 'apache2', { ensure => 'installed' })
```

By relying on this function instead of the preceding antipattern based around the `defined` function, you will avoid the unpredictable behavior of conflicting declarations. Instead, this will cause the compiler to fail when the declarations are passed to `ensure_resource`. This is still not a clean practice, though. Failed compilation is not a desirable alternative either.

Both functions should be avoided in favor of clean class structures with nonambiguous resource declarations.

Summary

A template is a frequent occurrence and is one of the best ways for Puppet to manage dynamic file content. Evaluating each template requires extra effort from the compiler, but the gain in flexibility is usually worth it.

The concept of virtual resources is much less ubiquitous. Virtual resources allow you to flexibly add certain entities to a node's catalog. The collector syntax that is used for this can also be used to override attribute values, which works even for nonvirtual resources as well.

Once PuppetDB is installed and configured, you can also export resources so that other node manifests can receive their configuration information. This allows you to model distributed systems quite elegantly.

The resource defaults are just a syntactic shortcut that help keep your manifest concise. They have to be used with care, though. Some language features such as the `defined` function (and its module-based successor, which is the `ensure_resource` function) should not be used at all.

The next chapter introduces an efficient way to handle differences among your managed nodes, both individually and in groups. It also finally resolves the problems that class parameterization can pose for your manifest designs.

7
Separating Data from Code Using Hiera

After working through the first six chapters, you now have quite a solid grasp on the principles of Puppet manifests. You have used the basic structural elements in numerous examples and contexts. There has even been a quick demonstration of the more advanced language features.

For all their expressive power, manifests do have some limitations. A manifest that is designed by the principles taught up to this point mixes logic with data. Logic is not only evident in control structures such as `if` and `else`, but it also just emerges from the network of classes and defines that include and instantiate one another.

However, you cannot configure a machine by just including some generic classes. Many properties of a given system are individual and must be passed as parameters. This can have maintenance implications for a manifest that must accommodate a large number of nodes. This chapter will teach you how to bring order back to such complex code bases by stepping through the following sections:

- Understanding the need for separate data storage
- Structuring configuration data in a hierarchy
- Retrieving and using Hiera values in manifests
- Converting resources to data
- Using Hiera from other contexts
- A practical example
- Debugging Hiera lookups

Understanding the need for separate data storage

Looking back at what you implemented during this book so far, you managed to create some very versatile code that did very useful things in an automatic fashion. Your nodes can distribute entries for /etc/hosts among themselves. They register each other's public SSH key for authentication. A node can automatically register itself to a central Cacti server.

Thanks to Facter, Puppet allows the effortless handling of these use cases. Many configuration items are unique to each node only because they refer to a detail (such as an IP address or a generated key) that is already defined. Sometimes, the required configuration data can be found on a remote machine only, which Puppet handles through exported resources. Such manifest designs that can rely on facts are very economic. The information has already been gathered, and a single class can most likely behave correctly for many or all of your nodes and manage a common task in a graceful manner.

However, some configuration tasks have to be performed individually for each node, and these can incorporate settings that are rather arbitrary and not directly derived from the node's existing properties:

- In a complex MySQL replication setup that spans multiple servers, each participant requires a unique server ID. Duplicates must be prevented under any circumstances, so randomly generating the ID numbers is not safe.

- Some of your networks might require regular maintenance jobs to be run from cron. If there must be no overlapping of the runs on any two machines, Puppet should define a starting time for each machine to ensure this.

- In server operations, you have to perform monitoring of the disk space usage on all systems. Most disks should generate early warnings so that there is time to react. However, other disks will be expected to be almost full at most times and should have a much higher warning threshold.

When custom-built systems and software are managed through Puppet, they are also likely to require this type of micromanagement for each instance. The examples here represent only a tiny slice of the things that Puppet must manage explicitly and independently.

Consequences of defining data in the manifest

There are a number of ways in which a Puppet manifest can approach this problem of micromanagement. The most direct way is to define whole sets of classes — one for each individual node:

```
class site::mysql_server01 {
    class { 'mysql': server_id => '1', … }
}
class site::mysql_server02 {
    class { 'mysql': server_id => '2', … }
}
…
class site::mysql_aux01 {
    class { 'mysql': server_id => '101', … }
}
# and so forth …
```

This is a very high-maintenance solution for the following reasons:

- The individual classes can become quite elaborate, because all required `mysql` class parameters have to be used in each one
- There is much redundancy among the parameters that are, in fact, identical among all nodes
- The individually different values can be hard to spot and must be carefully kept unique throughout the whole collection of classes
- This is only really feasible by keeping these classes close together, which might conflict with other organizational principles of your code base

In short, this is the brute-force approach that introduces its own share of cost. A more economic approach is to pass the values that are different among nodes from variables. The variable values are assigned right in each respective `node` block:

```
node 'xndp12-sql09' {
    $mysql_server_id = '103'
    include site::mysql_server
}
```

As the classes can now rely on individual variable values, you can make them general again:

```
class site::mysql_server {
    class {
        'mysql':
            server_id => $mysql_server_id,
            ...
    }
}
```

This is much better, because it eliminates the redundancy and its impact on maintainability. The wrinkle is that the node blocks can become quite messy with variable declarations for many different subsystems. Explanatory comments contribute to the wall of text that each node block can become.

You can take this a step further by defining lookup tables in hash variables, outside of any node or class, on the global scope:

```
$mysql_config_table = {
    'xndp12-sql01' => {
        server_id => '1',
        buffer_pool => '12G',
    },
    ...
}
```

This lifts the need to declare any variables in node blocks. The classes look up the values from the hash directly:

```
class site::mysql_server {
    $config = $mysql_config_table[$hostname]
    class {
        'mysql':
            server_id => $config['server_id'],
            ...
    }
}
```

This is pretty sophisticated and is actually close to the even better way that you will learn about in this chapter. Note that this approach still retains a leftover possibility for redundancy. Some configuration values are likely to be identical among all nodes that belong to one group, but are unique to each group (for example, preshared keys of any variety).

This requires that all servers in the mentioned `xndp12` cluster contain some key/value pairs that are identical for all members:

```
$crypt_key_xndp12 = 'xneFGl%23ndfAWLN34a0t9w30.zges4'
$config = {
    'xndp12-stor01' => { $crypt_key => $crypt_key_xndp12, … },
    'xndp12-stor02' => { $crypt_key => $crypt_key_xndp12, … },
    'xndp12-sql01'  => { $crypt_key => $crypt_key_xndp12, … },
    …
}
```

This is not ideal, but let's stop here. There is no point worrying about even more elaborate ways to sort configuration data into recursive hash structures. Such solutions will quickly grow very difficult to understand and maintain anyway. The silver bullet is an external database that holds all individual and shared values. Before I go into the details of using Hiera for just this purpose, let's discuss the general ideas of hierarchical data storage.

Structuring configuration data in a hierarchy

In the previous section, we reduced the data problem to a simple need for key/value pairs that are specific to each node under Puppet management. Puppet and its manifests then serve as the engine that generates actual configuration from these minimalistic bits of information.

A simplistic approach to this problem is an `ini` style configuration file that has a section for each node that sets values for all configurable keys. Shared values will be declared in one or more general sections:

```
[mysql]
buffer_pool=15G
log_file_size=500M
...
[xndp12-sql01]
psk=xneFGl%23ndfAWLN34a0t9w30.zges4
server_id=1
```

Rails applications customarily do something similar and store their configuration in a YAML format. The user can define different environments, such as `production`, `staging`, and `testing`. The values that are defined per environment override the global setting values.

This is quite close to the type of hierarchical configuration that Puppet allows through its Hiera binding. The hierarchies that the mentioned Rails applications and `ini` files achieve through configuration environments are quite flat—there is a global layer and an overlay for specialized configuration. With Hiera and Puppet, a single configuration database is required to handle whole clusters of machines and entire networks of such clusters. This implies a need for a more elaborate hierarchy.

Hiera allows you to define your own hierarchical layers. There are some typical, proven examples, which are found in many configurations out there:

1. The `common` layer holds default values for all agents
2. A `location` layer can override some values in accordance with the data center that houses each respective node
3. Each agent machine typically fills a distinct `role` in your infrastructure, such as `wordpress_appserver` or `puppetdb_server`
4. Some configuration is specific to each single `machine`.

For example, consider the configuration of a hypothetical reporting client. Your `common` layer will hold lots of presets such as default verbosity settings, the transport compression option, and other choices that should work for most machines. On the `location` layer, you ensure that each machine checks in to the respective local server—reporting should not use WAN resources.

Settings per role are perhaps the most interesting part. They allow fine-grained settings that are specific to a class of servers. Perhaps your application servers should monitor their memory consumption in very close intervals. For the database servers, you will want a closer view at hard drive operations and performance. For your Puppet servers, there might be special plugins that gather specific data.

The `machine` layer is very useful in order to declare any exceptions from the rule. There are always some machines that require special treatment for one reason or another. With a top hierarchy layer that holds data for each single agent, you get full control over all the data that an agent uses.

These ideas are still quite abstract, so let's finally look at the actual application of Hiera.

Configuring Hiera

The support for retrieving data values from Hiera has been built into Puppet since Version 3. All you need in order to get started is a `hiera.yaml` file in the configuration directory.

 Of course, the location and name of the configuration is customizable, as is almost everything that is related to configuration. Look for the `hiera_config` setting.

As the filename extension suggests, the configuration is in the YAML format and contains a hash with keys for the backends, the hierarchy, and backend-specific settings. The keys are noted as Ruby symbols with a leading colon:

```
:backends:
  - yaml
:hierarchy:
  - %{::clientcert}
  - role-%{::role}
  - at-%{::datacenter}
  - common
:yaml:
  :datadir: /etc/puppet/env/%{::environment}/hiera
```

Note that the value of `:backends` is actually a single element array. You can pick multiple backends. The significance will be explained later. The `:hierarchy` value key contains a list of the actual layers that were described earlier. Each entry is the name of a data source. When Hiera retrieves a value, it searches each data source in turn. The `%{}` expression allows you to access the values of Puppet variables. Use only facts or global scope variables here—anything else will make Hiera's behavior quite confusing.

 It was explained earlier that fact names need not be prepended with the `::` double colon anymore. In the Hiera configuration, however, this is still a good idea. Otherwise, a local variable that hides one of the used facts in the wrong place in the manifest can cause you many headaches.

Finally, you will need to include configurations for each of your backends. The mentioned configuration uses the YAML backend only, so there is only a hash for `:yaml` with the one supported `:datadir` key, which is where Hiera will expect to find YAML files with data. For each data source, the `datadir` key can contain one `.yaml` file. As the names of the sources are dynamic, you will typically create more than four or five data source files. Let's create some examples before we have a short discussion on the combination of multiple backends.

Storing Hiera data

The backend of your Hiera setup determines how you have to store your configuration values. For the YAML backend, you fill `datadir` with files that each hold a hash of values. Let's put some elements of the reporting engine configuration into the example hierarchy:

```
# /etc/puppet/env/production/hiera/common.yaml
reporting::server: stats01.example.net
reporting::server_port: 9033
```

The values in `common.yaml` are defaults that are used for all agents. They are at the broad base of the hierarchy. Values that are specific to a `location` or `role` apply to smaller groups of your agents. For example, the database servers of the `postgre` role should run some special reporting plugins:

```
# /etc/puppet/env/production/hiera/role-postgre.yaml
reporting::plugins:
   - iops
   - cpuload
```

On such a higher layer, you can also override the values from the lower layers. For example, a role-specific data source such as `role-postgre.yaml` can set a value for `reporting::server_port` as well. The layers are searched from the most to the least specific, and the first value is used. This is why it is a good idea to have a node-specific data source at the top of the hierarchy. On this layer, you can override any value for each agent. In this example, the reporting node can use the loopback interface to reach itself:

```
# /etc/puppet/env/production/hiera/stats01.example.net.yaml
reporting::server: localhost
```

Each agent receives a patchwork of configuration values according to the concrete YAML files that make up its specific hierarchy.

Don't worry if all this feels a bit overwhelming. There are more examples in this chapter. Hiera also has the charming characteristic that it can seem rather complicated on paper but feels very natural and intuitive once you try using it yourself.

Choosing your backends

There are three built-in backends: YAML, JSON, and Puppet. This chapter will focus on YAML, because it's a very convenient and efficient form of data notation. The JSON backend is very similar to YAML. It looks for data in .json files instead of .yaml for each data source; these files obviously use a different data notation format. With the puppet backend, you get to write Puppet manifests that declare variables that hold Hiera data. It's a good choice for users who don't see virtue in JSON nor YAML.

The use of multiple backends should never be truly necessary. In most cases, a well-thought-out hierarchy will suffice for your needs. With a second backend, data lookup will traverse your hierarchy once per backend. This means that the lowest level of your primary backend will rank higher than any layer from additional backends.

In some cases, it might be worthwhile to add another backend just to get the ability to define even more basic defaults in an alternative location—perhaps a distributed filesystem or a source control repository with different commit privileges.

Also, note that you can add custom backends to Hiera, so these might also be sensible choices for secondary or even tertiary backends. A Hiera backend is written in Ruby, like the Puppet plugins. The details of creating such a backend are beyond the scope of this book.

 Consult the online documentation at https://docs.puppetlabs.com/hiera/1/custom_backends.html if this topic is of interest to you.

You have studied the theory of storing data in Hiera at length, so it's finally time to see how to make use of this in Puppet.

Retrieving and using Hiera values in manifests

Looking up a key value in Hiera is easy. Puppet comes with a very straightforward function for this:

```
$plugins = hiera('reporting::plugins')
```

Whenever the compiler encounters such a call in the manifest of the current agent node, it triggers a search in the hierarchy. The specific data sources are determined by the fact values provided by the agent (if you rely on facts to define your hierarchy, of course, which is the most common and sensible way).

If the named key cannot be found in the agent's hierarchy, the master aborts the catalog compilation with an error. To prevent this, it is often sensible to supply a default value with the lookup:

```
$plugins = hiera('reporting::plugins', [])
```

In this case, Puppet uses an empty array if the hierarchy mentions no plugins.

Working with simple values

You have seen how to invoke the `hiera` function for value retrieval. There is really not more to it than what you have seen in the previous section, except for an optional parameter. It allows you to include an additional layer at the top of your hierarchy. If the key is found in the named data source, it will override the result from the regular hierarchy:

```
$plugins = hiera('reporting::plugins', [], 'global-overrides')
```

If the `reporting::plugins` key is found in the `global-overrides` data source, the value is taken from there. Otherwise, the normal hierarchy is searched.

Generally, assigning the retrieved value to a manifest variable is quite common. However, you can also invoke the `hiera` function in other useful contexts, such as the following:

```
@@cacti_device {
    $fqdn:
        ip => hiera('snmp_address', $ipaddress),
}
```

The lookup result can be handed to a resource directly as a parameter value. This is an example of how to allow Hiera to define a specific IP address per machine that should be used for a specific service. It acts as a simple way to manually override Facter's assumptions.

Another frequent occurrence is a parameter default that is made dynamic through a Hiera lookup:

```
define logrotate::config(
        $rotations = hiera('logrotate::rotations', 7)
        ) {
    # regular define code here
}
```

The Hiera value is ignored for all instances of `logrotate::config` that supply a value during their declaration. This can be a little confusing:

```
logrotate::config { '/var/log/cacti.log': rotations => 12 }
```

Still, the pattern adds some convenience. It also allows for the customization of resources that are declared inside modules:

```
vendor_module::config {
    file {
        '/etc/vendor_config':
            source => 'puppet:///modules/vendor_module/etc/vendor_
config',
            owner  => hiera('vendor_module::user', 'vendor_user'),
    }
}
```

Customizing the file owner will otherwise require an according parameter for the declaring class or an explicit override of the resource. Speaking of class parameters, Hiera has some special semantics that makes using them very convenient.

Binding class parameter values automatically

The concept of parameterized classes might have gotten a somewhat tarnished reputation, judging from my coverage of it so far. It allegedly makes it difficult to include classes from multiple places in the manifest or silently allows it under shifting circumstances. While that is true, you can avoid these issues by relying on Hiera for your class parameterization needs.

Since Puppet Version 3.2, it has been possible to choose the values for any class' parameters right in the Hiera data. Whenever you include a class that has any parameters, Puppet will query Hiera to find a value for each of them. The keys must be named after the class and parameter names, joined by a double colon. Remember the `cacti` class from *Chapter 5*, *Extending Your Puppet Infrastructure with Modules*? It had a `$redirect` parameter. To define its value in Hiera, add the `cacti::redirect` key:

```
# cacti01.example.net.yaml
cacti::redirect: false
```

Some classes have very elaborate interfaces — the `apache` class from the Puppet Labs module accepts 49 parameters at the time of writing this. If you need many of those, you can put them into your machine's dedicated YAML file as one coherent block of keys with values. It will be quite readable, because the `apache::` prefixes line up.

You don't save any lines compared to specifying them right in the manifest, but at least the wall of options will not get in your way while you're programming in your manifests—you separated data from code.

The point that is perhaps the most redeeming for class parameterization is that each key is independent in your hierarchy. Many parameters can most likely be defined for many or all of your machines. Clusters of application servers can share some settings (if your hierarchy includes a layer on which they are grouped together), and you can override parameters for single machines as you see fit:

```
# common.yaml
apache::default_ssl_cert: /var/lib/puppet/ssl/certs/%{fqdn}.pem
apache::default_ssl_key: /var/lib/puppet/ssl/private_keys/%{fqdn}.pem
apache::purge_configs: false
```

Your site is prepared to use the Puppet certificates for HTTPS. This is a good choice for internal services, because trust to Puppet CA can be easily established, and the certificates are available on all agent machines. Also, the module should generally not obliterate any existing or manually added Apache configuration controlled by the purge_configs flag:

```
# role-httpsec.yaml
apache::purge_configs: true
apache::server_tokens: Minimal
apache::server_signature: off
apache::trace_enable: off
```

Machines that have the httpsec role override this setting—the Apache configuration should be purged so that it matches the managed configuration completely. The hierarchy of such machines also defines some additional values that are not defined in the common layer.

A specific machine's YAML can override keys from either layer if need be:

```
# sec02-sxf12.yaml
apache::default_ssl_cert: /opt/ssl/custom.pem
apache::default_ssl_key: /opt/ssl/custom.key
apache::trace_enable: extended
```

All these settings require no additional work. They take effect automatically, provided that the apache class from the puppetlabs-apache module is included.

For some users, this might be the only way in which Hiera is employed on their master, which is perfectly valid. You can even design your manifests specifically to expose all configurable items as class parameters. However, keep in mind that another advantage of Hiera is that any value can be retrieved from many different places in your manifest.

For example, if your firewalled servers are reachable through dedicated NAT ports, you will want to add this port to each machine's Hiera data. The manifest can export this value not only to the firewall server itself, but also to external servers that use it in scripts and configurations to reach the exporting machine:

```
$nat_port = hiera('site::net::nat_port')
@@firewall {
    "650 forward port $nat_port to $fqdn":
        proto       => 'tcp',
        dport       => $nat_port,
        destination => hiera('site::net::nat_ip'),
        jump        => 'DNAT',
        todest => $ipaddress,
        tag         => hiera('site::net::firewall_segment'),
}
```

The values will most likely be defined on different hierarchical layers. The nat_port is agent-specific and can only be defined in the %{::fqdn} (or %{::clientcert} for better security) data source. The nat_ip is probably identical for all servers in the same cluster. They might share a server role. The firewall_segment could well be identical for all servers that share the same location:

```
# stor03.example.net.yaml
site::net::nat_port: 12020
...
# role-storage.yaml
site::net::nat_ip: 198.58.119.126
...
# location-portland.yaml
site::net::firewall_segment: segment04
...
```

As previously mentioned, some of this data will be helpful in other contexts as well. Assume that you deploy a script through a defined type. The script sends messages to remote machines. The destination address and port are passed to the defined type as parameters. Each node that should be targeted can export this script resource:

```
@@site::maintenance_script {
    "/usr/local/bin/maint-$fqdn":
```

```
        address => hiera('site::net::nat_ip'),
        port    => hiera('site::net::nat_port'),
    }
```

It would be impractical to do all this in one class that takes the port and address as parameters. You would want to retrieve the same value from within different classes or even modules, each taking care of the respective exports.

Handling hashes and arrays

Some examples in this chapter defined array values in Hiera. The good news is that retrieving arrays and hashes from Hiera is not at all different from simple strings, numbers, or Boolean values. The `hiera` function will return all these values, which are ready for use in the manifest.

There are two more functions that offer special handling for such values: the `hiera_array` and `hiera_hash` functions.

> The presence of these functions can be somewhat confusing. New users might assume that these are required whenever retrieving hashes or arrays from the hierarchy. When inheriting Puppet code, it can be a good idea to double-check that these derived functions are actually used correctly in a given context.

When the `hiera_array` function is invoked, it gathers all named values from the whole hierarchy and merges them into one long array that comprises all elements that were found. Take the distributed firewall configuration once more, for example. Each node should be able to export a list of rules that open ports for public access. The manifest for this would be completely driven by Hiera:

```
if hiera('site::net::nat_ip', false) {
    @@firewall {
        "200 NAT ports for $fqdn":
            port        => hiera_array('site::net::nat_ports'),
            proto       => 'tcp',
            destination => hiera('site::net::nat_ip'),
            jump        => 'DNAT',
            todest      => $ipaddress,
    }
}
```

Note the seemingly nonsensical default value of `false` for the `site::net::nat_ip` key in the `if` clause. This forms a useful pattern, though—the resource should only be exported if `public_ip` is defined for the respective node.

Care must be taken if `false` or the empty string is a conceivable value for the key in question. In this case, the `if` clause will ignore that value. In such cases, you should use a well-defined comparison instead:

```
if hiera('feature_flag_A', undef) != undef { … }
```

The hierarchy can then hold ports on several layers:

```
# common.yaml
nat_ports: 22
```

The SSH port should be available for all nodes that get a public address. Note that this value is not an array itself. This is fine; Hiera will include scalar values in the resulting list without any complaint.

```
# role-webserver.yaml
nat_ports: [ 80, 443 ]
```

Standalone web application servers present their HTTP and HTTPS ports to the public.

```
# tbt-backend-test.example.net.yaml
nat_ports:
  - 5973
  - 5974
  - 5975
  - 6630
```

The testing instance for your new cloud service should expose a range of ports for custom services. If it has the `webserver` role (somehow), it will lead to an export of ports `22`, `80`, and `443` as well as its individually chosen list.

 When designing such a construct, keep in mind that the array merge is only ever-cumulative. There is no way to exclude values that were added in lower layers from the final result. In this example, you will have no opportunity to disable the SSH port `22` for any given machine. You should take good care when adding common values.

A similar alternative lookup function exists for hashes. The `hiera_hash` function also traverses the whole hierarchy and constructs a hash by merging all hashes it finds under the given Hiera key from all hierarchy layers. Hash keys in higher layers overwrite those from lower layers. All values must be hashes. Strings, arrays, or other data types are not allowed in this case:

```
# common.yaml
haproxy_settings:
```

```
log_socket: /dev/log
log_level: info
user: haproxy
group: haproxy
daemon: true
```

These are the default settings for `haproxy` at the lowest hierarchy level. On web servers, the daemon should run as the general web service user:

```
# role-webserver.yaml
haproxy_settings:
  user: www-data
  group: www-data
```

When retrieved using `hiera('haproxy_settings')`, this will just evaluate to the hash, `{ 'user' => 'www-data', 'group' => 'www-data' }`. The hash at the role-specific layer completely overrides the default settings.

To get all values, create a merger using `hiera_hash('haproxy_settings')` instead. The result is likely to be more useful:

```
{ 'log_socket' => '/dev/log', 'log_level' => 'info',
  'user' => 'www-data', 'group' => 'www-data', 'daemon' => true }
```

The limitations are similar to those of `hiera_array`. Keys from any hierarchy level cannot be removed, they can only be overwritten with different values. The end result is quite similar to what you would get from replacing the hash with a group of keys:

```
# role-webserver.yaml
haproxy::user: www-data
haproxy::group: www-data
```

If you opt to do this, the data can also be easily fit to a class that can bind these values to parameters automatically. Preferring flat structures can, therefore, be beneficial. Defining hashes in Hiera is still generally worthwhile, as the next section explains.

Converting resources to data

You can now move configuration settings to Hiera and dedicate your manifest to logic. This works very seamlessly as far as classes and their parameters are concerned, because class parameters automatically retrieve their values from Hiera. For configuration that requires you to instantiate resources, you still need to write the full manifests and add manual lookup function calls.

For example, an Apache web server requires some global settings, but the interesting parts of its configuration are typically performed in virtual host configuration files. Puppet models them with defined resource types. If you want to configure an `iptables` firewall, you have to declare lots of resources of the `firewall` type (available through the `puppetlabs-firewall` module).

Such elaborate resources can clutter up your manifest, yet they mostly represent data. There is no inherent logic to many firewall rules, although a set of rules is derived from one or several key values sometimes. Virtual hosts often stand for themselves as well, with little or no relation to configuration details that are relevant to other parts of the setup.

Puppet comes with yet another function that allows you to move whole sets of such resources to Hiera data. The pattern is straightforward: a group of resources of the same type are represented by a hash. The keys are resource titles, and the values are yet another layer of hashes with key/value pairs for attributes:

```
services:
  apache2:
    enable: true
    ensure: running
  syslog-ng:
    enable: false
```

This YAML data represents two `service` resources. To make Puppet add them as actual resources to the catalog, pass the hash to the `create_resources` function:

```
create_resources('service', hiera('services', {}))
```

The first argument is the name of the resource type, and the second must be the hash of actual resources. The created resources honor resource defaults for the given type:

```
Service { require => Mount['/var/run'] }
```

In addition, you can also pass an additional hash with default parameter names and values as the third parameter to `create_resources`. This can help keep your resource hashes compact:

```
create_resources('file', hiera('synced_directories'),
    { ensure => 'directory', recurse => true, mode => 640 })
```

The defaults save you two to three lines per YAML resource:

```
synced_directories:
  /etc/apache2/conf.d:
    source: puppet:///modules/sneeze_app/etc/apache2/conf.d
```

```
    mode: 644
/var/lib/sneeze/config:
    source: puppet:///modules/sneeze_app/config
    group: www-data
```

The data is more maintainable this way, although it is a bit more difficult to discern what attribute values each created resource will use. It is, of course, sensible to include the default hash in the Hiera data as well:

```
synced_directories_defaults:
    ensure: directory
    recurse: true
    mode: 640
```

In theory, this allows you to move almost all your code to Hiera data. (The next section discusses how desirable that really is.) There is one more feature that goes step further in this direction:

```
hiera_include('classes')
```

This call gathers values from all over the hierarchy, just like `hiera_array`. The resulting array is interpreted as a list of class names. All these named classes are included. This allows for some additional consolidation in your manifest:

```
# common.yaml
classes:
    - ssh
    - syslog
...
# role-webserver.yaml
classes:
    - apache
    - logrotate
    - syslog
```

You can possibly even use `hiera_include` to declare these classes outside of any `node` block. The data will then affect all nodes. Additionally, from some distinct classes, you might also declare other classes via `hiera_include`, whose names are stored under a different Hiera key.

> The ability to enumerate classes for each node to include is what Puppet's **External Node Classifiers** (**ENCs**) had originally been conceived for. Hiera can serve as a basic ENC thanks to the `hiera_include` function. This is most likely preferred over writing a custom ENC. However, it should be noted that some open source ENCs such as Foreman are quite powerful and can add much convenience; Hiera has not supplanted the concept as a whole.

The combination of these tools opens some ways for you to shrink your manifests to their essential parts and configure your machines gracefully through Hiera.

Choosing between manifest and Hiera designs

You can now move most of the concrete configuration to the data storage. Classes can be included from the manifest or through Hiera. Puppet looks up parameter values in the hierarchy, and you can flexibly distribute the configuration values there in order to achieve just the desired result for each node with minimal effort and redundancy.

This does not mean that you don't write actual manifest code anymore. The manifest is still the central pillar of your design. You will often need logic that uses the configuration data as input. For example, there might be classes that should only be included if a certain value is retrieved from Hiera:

```
if hiera('use_caching_proxy', false) {
    include nginx
}
```

If you try and rely on Hiera exclusively, you will have to add nginx to the classes array at all places in the hierarchy that set the use_caching_proxy flag to true. This is prone to mistakes. What's worse is that the flag can be overridden from true to false at a more specific layer, but the nginx element cannot be removed from an array that is retrieved by hiera_include.

It is important to keep in mind that the manifest and data should compliment each other. Build manifests primarily and add lookup function calls at opportune places. Defining flags and values in Hiera should allow you (or the user of your modules) to alter the behavior of the manifest. The data should not be the driver of the catalog composition, except for places in which you replace large numbers of static resources with large data structures.

Using Hiera in different contexts

You will most likely find yourself in need of some data from Hiera when designing templates for configuration or other files. For example, when building your personal module in order to manage the SSH server, you might want to allow nodes to specify a list of environment variables for the AcceptEnv option.

Granted, this will most likely be passed as a parameter to a class within such a module. The Hiera data will just be bound to the parameter and be available to the template as a regular Puppet variable. Let's ignore this just to have a contrived example for data retrieval from a template.

The naïve implementation would not work inside the template:

```
<% # pseudo code!
   vars = hiera('ssh::server::env_vars', [ 'LANG', 'LC_*' ]) -%>
AcceptEnv = <%= vars * ' ' %>
```

The issue is that this call will be directed at a `hiera` method in Ruby and not the Puppet function. Templates have a way of accessing Puppet's parser functions, but it takes just a little more writing. The Ruby code has to access the local `scope` attribute, which has a method for each parser function. These methods add a `function_` prefix to the parser function name:

```
<% vars = scope.function_hiera('ssh::server::env_vars', …) -%>
AcceptEnv = <%= vars * ' ' %>
```

This holds true for all functions, such as `split`, `md5`, and all other functions that you can use from the manifest. However, like the two functions mentioned, most of these have Ruby equivalents. They are often more powerful or convenient. Hiera does have a Ruby binding, of course. However, in this case, the Puppet function is more convenient, because it implicitly adds all parameters that Hiera requires in order to build the calling agent's individual hierarchy.

It's not quite accurate to state that Hiera also has a Ruby binding. Hiera consists mainly of a Ruby library. The more fitting description is that Hiera also has a Puppet binding through the `hiera` functions.

The other Ruby context that you might encounter is parser functions. The limitations of template code apply here as well. You cannot just call the Puppet function as `hiera()`. The solution is slightly different from the one in templates, because the function code can access methods of the `scope` attribute directly. In the function body, you only need to add the `function_` prefix:

```
data = function_hiera('key', 'default')
```

This is somewhat more rare than the template case—your own functions will most likely receive data from Hiera (or any source) through their own parameters and have no need to look it up themselves.

You might have noticed that I did not mention types and providers—they consist of Ruby code as well, as do facts. The big difference is that all these pieces of code are not run during the compilation. This is why they do not have access to the hierarchy of data that is stored on the master.

A practical example

To round things off, let's build a complete example of a module that is enhanced with Hiera. Create a `demo` module in the environment of your choice. I will go with `production`:

```
# /etc/puppet/env/production/modules/demo/manifests/init.pp
class demo($auto = false,
          $syslog = true,
          $user = 'nobody') {
    file { '/usr/local/bin/demo': ... }
    if $auto {
        cron { 'auto-demo':
            user    => $user,
            command => '/usr/local/bin/demo'
            ...
        }
        create_resources('demo::atom', hiera('demo::atoms', {})
    }
}
```

This class implicitly looks up three Hiera keys for its parameters:

- `demo::auto`
- `demo::syslog`
- `demo::user`

There is also an explicit lookup of an optional `demo::atoms` hash that creates configuration items for the module. Each hash must fit the defined type, which is `demo::atom`, so that sensible resources can be created:

```
# /etc/puppet/env/production/modules/demo/manifests/atom.pp
define demo::atom($address, $port=14193) {
    file { "/etc/demo.d/$name":
        ensure  => 'file',
        content => "---\nhost: $address\nport: $port\n",
        mode    => '644',
        owner   => 'root',
```

```
        group    => 'root',
    }
}
```

The module uses a default of `nobody` for `user`. Your site does not run scripts with this account, so you set your preference in `common.yaml`. You also don't commonly use `syslog`:

```
demo::user: automation
demo::syslog: false
```

As this user account is restricted on your guest workstations, Hiera should set an alternative value in `role-public_desktop.yaml`:

```
demo::user: maintenance
```

Cron jobs are usually managed in site modules but not for web servers. Let the `demo` module itself take care of this on web servers through the `$auto` parameter. The exception is `int01-web01.example.net`, where no cron jobs whatsoever should be scheduled:

```
# role-webserver.yaml
demo::auto: true
```

This is how to define the exception:

```
# int01-web01.example.net.yaml
demo::auto: false
```

Concerning configuration resources, each machine should add itself as a peer:

```
# common.yaml
demo::atoms:
  self:
    address: localhost
```

The Kerberos servers should not try this:

```
# role-kerberos.yaml
demo::atoms: {}
```

The database servers should also contact the custom server running on the Puppet master machine on a nonstandard port:

```
# role-dbms.yaml
demo::atoms:
  self:
```

```
        address: localhost
    master:
        address: master.example.net
        port: 60119
```

You can now include the `demo` class from your `site.pp` (or an equivalent) file indiscriminately. It is often a good idea to be able to allow certain agent machines to opt out of this behavior in the future. Just add an optional Hiera flag for this:

```
# site.pp
if hiera('enable_demo', true) {
    include demo
}
```

Agents that must not include the module can be given a `false` value for the `enable_demo` key in their data now.

Debugging Hiera lookups

As you can see from the preceding example, the data that contributes to the complete configuration of any module can be rather dispersed throughout the set of your data sources. It can be challenging to determine where the respective values are retrieved from for any given agent node. It can be frustrating to trace data sources to find out why a change at some level will not take effect for some of your agents.

To help make the process more transparent, Hiera comes with a command-line tool called `hiera`. Invoking it is simple:

```
$ hiera -c /etc/puppet/hiera.yaml demo::atoms
```

It retrieves a given key using the specified configuration from `hiera.yaml`. Make sure that you use the same Hiera configuration as Puppet.

Of course, this can only work sensibly if Hiera selects the same data sources as the compiler, which uses fact values to form a concrete hierarchy. These required facts can be given right on the command line as the final parameters:

```
$ hiera -c /etc/puppet/hiera.yaml demo::atoms \
    clientcert=int01-web01.example.net role=webserver location=ny
```

This prints the `demo::atoms` value of the specified server to the console. Make sure that you add the `-d` flag in order to get helpful information about the traversal of the hierarchy:

```
$ hiera -d -c ...
```

Summary

While Puppet manifests are a powerful tool to model relations of subsystems and dependencies among both single resources and whole groups, it is sensible to strip the concrete configuration data from them, at least in part. This helps consolidate your classes and allows you to avoid a cluttered code base.

Hiera is a tool that stores and retrieves data in a hierarchical fashion. Each retrieval uses a distinct data source from each hierarchy layer and traverses it from the most to the least specific. The first value that is found is returned. From Puppet, you will mainly perform lookups through the `hiera` function. The data sources are selected from a predefined hierarchy, which will rely on fact values in most cases. Data is commonly represented in YAML or JSON.

Another common way to employ Hiera through Puppet is to name the Hiera keys in the `<class-name>::<parameter-name>` format. When including a parameterized class, Puppet will look for such keys in Hiera and automatically bind the values to the parameters.

Manifests that boast large numbers of static resources can be cleaned up by converting the declarations to hashes and using the `create_resources` function to declare resources from the data. The hash conversion is easy, especially to YAML, because in this notation, the hash closely resembles the Puppet manifest syntax.

The next chapter combines much of what you have learned so far and enhances it with some ideas in order to get you started with your own manifest designs. Read on to acquire some more tools and patterns in order to use Puppet as an efficient cloud manager.

8
Configuring Your Cloud Application with Puppet

Up till this point, you have built quite a respectable basis of theoretic knowledge about the Puppet system. You now understand the nature of resources with their properties and parameters. You learned how the agent relates to the master and how Facter cooperates with them. The toolchain of types and providers has been explained, and you can even extend Puppet through your own custom plugins. Designing and structuring manifests through classes, defined types, and modules is becoming natural to you, and you have some more advanced language tools at your disposal as well.

It is now time to look from a more practical angle. Let's take a look at designs that are useful in common real-world scenarios. With the general trend of cloud computing, we will focus on some techniques that cater especially to the use of Puppet in cloud environments. This will not be limited to the manifest and module design; you will also learn some generally useful configuration and deployment techniques.

These are the topics that we'll cover in this final chapter:

- Typical scopes of Puppet
- Taking Puppet to the cloud
- Building manifests for the cloud
- Preparing for autoscaling
- Ensuring successful provisioning

Typical scopes of Puppet

Puppet was originally conceived for the automation and centralized maintenance of server configurations. As the community grew, Puppet developed some additional facets during its progression, and this trend will most likely continue. At the time of writing this, Puppet is viable for quite different purposes and different user groups.

The ability to write and share simple, one-shot manifests makes Puppet a good choice for all computer technicians. Development, quality assurance, operations, or any other field—they all can rely on Puppet. It allows them to not only document system requirements for specific tasks, but also implement a high-level "script" to enforce these requirements, perhaps even on different platforms.

> I used the term script here even though Puppet manifests should not be regarded as such. However, at the level of sharing small pieces of code to manage some very specific system details, they serve the same purpose as shared scripts. Note that in some cases, scripts serve better than manifests. This is most evident when the manifest comprises lots of chained exec type resources. Puppet is the more powerful choice when other native resources can be used—a manifest can then be simpler and more flexible than a shell script.

Another use case for Puppet that is ever growing in popularity is the provisioning of **Vagrant** instances. Vagrant is a tool that allows development teams to streamline the creation of development boxen in the form of managed virtual machines. It is a must-have for software teams that struggle with complicated setup routines for their testing environments. Vagrant comes with support that integrates Puppet manifests and modules right in the provisioning process of these VM instances.

That said, the majority of Puppet installations are most likely still performed with the intent of managing networks of machines, with a focus on servers and compute nodes in data centers. Some sites will also manage desktops through Puppet. This can be sensible in a large network with complex requirements for workstations.

Concerning OS platforms, Puppet is still primarily used on Linux-based systems, systems of the Debian or Red Hat family in particular. Other Linux flavors and BSDs are not as common but are readily supported. Windows support is also steadily progressing, as is the adoption of Puppet on this platform.

Outside of general-purpose servers, Puppet will also manage dedicated network components such as switches, routers, and other smart hardware. You can refer to http://puppetlabs.com/blog/puppet-network-device-management for more information.

Common data center use – roles and profiles

When managing whole networks with Puppet, efficiency is always among the primary goals. You will always be busy trying to avoid code redundancy where it is not required. By consolidating repetitive cases into common classes, you can minimize the maintenance overhead in the future. Of course, this works best if there is a system or pattern that directs the fashion in which such unification is to be performed and expected.

A very successful and widespread design pattern to this end was conceived by Craig Dunn and is called the **Roles and Profiles pattern**. It defines two layers of abstraction. The outer layer is roles, which are defined in a way that allows each server (or workstation) to choose exactly one role. There is no mixing—if a node has aspects of two different roles, then this merger forms a new role itself. Examples for roles can be `internal_webserver`, `key_distribution_center`, or `accounting_desktop`.

Technically, a role is just a class. It is sensible to organize your roles in a `role` or `roles` module:

```
node falstaff {
    include role::key_distribution_center
}
```

The design goal is to limit each `node` block to include just one role class. There should be no further `include` statements and no resource declarations. Variable declarations will be acceptable, but Hiera is almost universally preferred.

As for roles, they should comprise nothing but the inclusion of one or more profile classes. Profiles quite distinctly represent aspects of a system. In the server realm, typical profiles would be `apache_server`, `nginx_proxy`, `postgres_server`, or `ldap_master`. Just like roles, profiles should be organized in a dedicated module:

```
class role::key_distribution_center {
    include profile::heimdal_server
    include profile::firewall_internal
}
```

Profiles themselves will ideally just include a selection of modules with data from Hiera. In a `profile` class, it might also be acceptable to pass some module parameters directly in the manifest. A profile can consistently configure some of its required modules this way, without the need for possible redundancy in the Hiera data of all the nodes that use this profile.

This is risky, though, because profiles can become incompatible or even impose subtle evaluation-order dependencies. Having a Hiera layer is cleaner, as it selects data sources through each node's role. At this layer, you can cleanly express a new configuration that should be effective for all nodes that fill this role:

```
class profile::heimdal_server {
    include heimdal
    class { 'ssh': restricted => true }
}
```

This is just a very rough sketch of the principles behind the Roles and Profiles pattern. Craig has put up a comprehensive description on his blog, and the design has since been adopted by many users.

Taking Puppet to the cloud

It's time to finally talk about the cloud, which I managed to avoid when describing the different use cases. We will focus on the **Infrastructure as a Service (IaaS)** paradigm. These IaaS clouds consist of a network of virtual machines connected to the Internet. Each machine runs a basic operating system, which is chosen by the administrator.

> If you need a **Platform as a Service (PaaS)** implementation, read on to learn how you can practically implement your own PaaS system on top of an IaaS cloud using Puppet.

From Puppet's point of view, an IaaS cloud is not much different from a data center. After all, this kind of cloud was conceived to serve as a stand-in for physical data centers. It just replaces rack-mounted servers with virtual machines, along with virtualized network connections.

Of course, managing IaaS instances poses some unique challenges when compared to a local data center. Normally, the IT staff can freely choose all properties for each system that gets deployed. Cloud instances are usually not as thoroughly customized. The following sections will give you some pointers that can help you tackle the consequences.

Initializing agents in the cloud

Many things that concern system configuration and maintenance can be solved in more than one way. Initializing cloud instances with working Puppet agents is no exception. The most straightforward way is to do everything manually and treat the new IaaS virtual machine like any new Linux host that has received a base installation. You create the cloud instance from a Linux base image, connect via SSH, and walk through the steps in order to install Puppet, connect to the master, and order the certificate.

Of course, it is always a goal to manage your cloud with little manual intervention. Puppet itself should help you take control of your instances without issuing actual commands on their shells. Toward that end, it will be helpful to create an image that comes with preinstalled Puppet packages. However, this is only half the work at best—the agent still requires a trusted certificate in order to work effectively.

Performing all of the necessary operations in a fully automated fashion is not strictly required. If you need your cloud to support autoscaling, you will need to devise a way for Puppet to initialize new agents without any manual intervention. There is a whole section devoted to the topic of autoscaling (*Preparing for autoscaling*) later in this chapter. For now, let's keep things more simple.

Including the Puppet software in your base image eases the initialization. To take this a big step further, you can add a start-up script that makes the Puppet agent receive its certificate as soon as possible. This is best done using the agent's `--waitforcert` option. Normally, the agent will terminate after submitting its CSR to the master. Each subsequent run will immediately abort as well, until the master offers a signed certificate. Through defining a `waitforcert` interval, you instruct the agent to keep running instead. It will poll the master in the specified interval and cache the certificate once it becomes available.

With this, you can make your new instances request certificates and stand by until you sign them on the master with a simple shell script:

```
#!/bin/bash
export PATH=/bin:/usr/bin
CERT=`puppet agent --configprint certname`
DIR=`puppet agent --configprint certdir`
[ -f "${DIR}/${CERT}.pem" ] && exit 0
puppet agent --onetime --no-daemonize --waitforcert 300
```

If the certificate has already been received, the script terminates immediately, without running the Puppet agent. To make it run once the instance boots up, you can add it as a job in a file in /etc/cron.d/:

```
@reboot /usr/local/bin/receive-puppet-cert
```

It is still up to you to sign the certificates in the usual fashion using puppet cert on the master machine. This is good security, after all. Requests might be issued by rogue agents. Even if your master is firewalled, attackers might still be able to connect from a reused IP address or other vectors, depending on your firewall settings.

If your cloud workflow is based around your provider's web interface, you will most likely want to sign certificates through a web form as well. If you want this capability, you can install **Puppet Dashboard** on the master.

> The dashboard has been discontinued and receives community support only at this point. A more official version is available through Puppet Enterprise. The new web consoles, which are **PuppetBoard** and **Puppet Explorer**, are primarily frontends for PuppetDB and offer no support for signing certificates.

Using Puppet's cloud-provisioner module

Puppet Enterprise comes with a CLI that allows you to manage cloud instances driven by AWS, GCE, or VMware. You can add much the same capabilities to the community version by installing the puppetlabs-cloud_provisioner module. It only lacks VMware support.

What the module adds to Puppet is not a type or provider or even special manifest support. It makes new subcommands available.

> Puppet refers to subcommands such as agent, master, or cert as **Faces**.

These new Puppet Faces are specific to the respective cloud providers—you get similar families of commands under puppet node_aws and puppet node_gce. Once configured, you can get a listing of your EC2 instances:

```
puppet node_aws list
```

There are more actions besides `list` that allow you to create and terminate instances and perform other useful administrative tasks. As such, the cloud provisioner can stand in as a unified cross-platform alternative to the providers' own CLI offerings.

Building manifests for the cloud

One of the most significant operational differences between cloud-based systems and hardware on premises is the fact that you don't get to name your nodes. Server names are often chosen in a mnemonic fashion and communicate the machine's function. In the cloud, your network consists of a collection of anonymous work horses instead.

Enforcing a naming scheme will actually defeat parts of the purpose of a cloud system. The absence of order liberates you from quite some planning overhead that you have to take in your data center, where any node that you deploy must be fit into the greater scheme. Instead, you can add and remove nodes at any time, and the disordered cloud structure just adjusts.

The following sections deal with strategies that allow Puppet to operate under these conditions and with which Puppet actually helps you set up and maintain such an environment efficiently.

Mapping functionalities to nodes

With the generic naming of cloud instances, the usual methods of assigning manifests to nodes are not a good fit at all. Defining individual `node` blocks somewhere in your code base is hardly feasible:

```
node 'ec2-107-22-79-148.compute-1.amazonaws.com' {
    include role::cache_proxy
}
node 'ec2-107-22-110-102.compute-1.amazonaws.com' {
    include role::appserver
}
```

Defining role mappings in individual Hiera data sources would be equally troublesome. It is not a technical problem, of course, but it also hardly eases management or helps abstraction from the cloud layout beneath your services. This is especially obvious when facing the deletion and recommissioning of cloud instances—you will always be chasing old and new node names and keeping your manifests up to date.

Under the special circumstances of the cloud infrastructure, it is actually preferable to allow the Puppet agent to declare its target state itself. As always, the communication of such information to the master is implemented in the form of Facter facts. For example, you can add a custom fact called `my_cloud_app_role` that will choose the role for the respective agent.

 This is usually a bad design practice. Under most circumstances, you would want the master to be in full control of the manifests. The agent should not have free choice as to what its catalog should contain. This cloud design is an exception to this rule.

A very simple and direct way to add such a fact is to define an appropriate environment variable for the agent to read:

```
FACTER_my_cloud_app_role=appserver puppet agent --test
# or
export FACTER_my_cloud_app_role=appserver
puppet agent --test
```

Doing this consistently is most likely at least as much work as just adding an external fact to the respective instance:

```
# /etc/facter/facts.d/my_cloud_app_role.txt
my_cloud_app_role=appserver
```

The master expects a value that corresponds to an existing role and selects it from the role's module:

```
node default {
    include "role::${my_cloud_app_role}"
}
```

This design will do its job just fine. You don't need to create a dedicated image for each role (doing so partly defeats the purpose of managing your services with Puppet). The external fact is simple enough to make an initialization script handle its creation:

```
gcloud compute instances create instance1502 \
    --image debian-7 \
    --metadata startup-script='#!/bin/bash
        echo my_cloud_app_role=appserver \
                >/etc/facter/facts.d/role.txt'
```

This makes it easy to rapidly deploy instances to fill a specified role. However, there is one wrinkle in this scheme. I mentioned previously how it is generally undesirable to allow agents to choose their own manifest. One reason for this is that it leaves you open to failure scenarios in which a given machine (perhaps inadvertently) suddenly chooses a foreign role at an unexpected point in time. The results can be hard to predict, because your manifests are most likely not tailored to enable the switch from one role to another. As a result, the affected machine might start running services for different roles, some of which use an incomplete or inconsistent configuration.

There is an alternative to regular facts that avoids this kind of trouble. An agent can register some values with the master during certificate generation already. These fact values are included in extension fields of the certificate itself and are hence approved by the master. From this point on, the master can trust these values to be truthful, because the agent cannot alter them once the certificate is signed. This is why this facility is known as **Trusted Facts**. Enable them on the master by setting the `trusted_node_data=true` option in the `puppet.conf` file.

 This is quite a new feature. Be sure to use a recent version of Puppet that is higher than 3.5.

Each trusted fact value is indexed with an OID from either the `1.3.6.1.4.1.34380.1.1` or `.2` subtrees. The first four OIDs in the former range are registered for typical use cases with Puppet:

- `Puppet Node UUID 1.3.6.1.4.1.34380.1.1.1`

- `Puppet Node Instance ID 1.3.6.1.4.1.34380.1.1.2`

- `Puppet Node Image Name 1.3.6.1.4.1.34380.1.1.3`

- `Puppet Node Preshared Key 1.3.6.1.4.1.34380.1.1.4`

These do not really fit the use case of defining the node's role, so it makes sense to pick a custom OID, such as `1.3.6.1.4.1.34380.1.2.42`. To define a value that should permanently become part of the agent's certificate, add the OID to `/etc/puppet/csr_attributes.yaml`:

```
---
extension_requests:
    1.3.6.1.4.1.34380.1.2.42: appserver
```

This data must be supplied before the Puppet agent generates its CSR for the master. The key/value pair is then applied to the request. On the master side, no additional steps are required in order to include the data into the signed certificate. The usual `puppet cert sign` command suffices.

With the certificate containing this persistent value, the master can safely derive the agent node's role from this Trusted Fact:

```
$role = $trusted['extensions']['1.3.6.1.4.1.34380.1.2.42']
node default {
    include "role::$role"
}
```

> Again, this pattern is not adequate for general Puppet use. The value is immutable, so if a change of roles is necessary, it requires the signing of a new certificate. This can happen if you need to subdivide an existing role into more specific derivatives. Under the cloud paradigm, this is less problematic—you will just recommission the affected instances anyway.

Choosing certificate names

We have now established that (unlike more traditional Puppet setups) the certificate name is of no consequence to the role that each cloud instance will fill. It follows that the certificate's common name can be chosen arbitrarily, because there should be no other configuration that depends on a sensible name. Under the cloud paradigm, it makes no sense to use the `fqdn` or `clientcert` facts in your Hiera hierarchy. If your cloud instances need individually different configuration data, even among nodes with the same role, you are probably facing a basic design problem.

As a cloud instance's DNS name is also quite arbitrary, you can just make Puppet use it as the certificate name. This poses a problem, though: as instances get decommissioned and recommissioned, their IP addresses and DNS names can repeat themselves. In other words, a new instance can end up with the same connectivity details as a former instance that you have used in the past.

This is problematic because the master keeps an inventory of signed certificates. When a new agent issues a CSR for a certificate that has been signed for a different agent in the past, the master has to assume that someone is impersonating the original agent. It will refuse to accept the CSR.

> This is especially dangerous when autoscaling is in use. Agent provisioning has to run unattended, and both deletion and creation of instances is a relatively frequent occurrence.

It is, therefore, safer to go the extra mile and create a UUID for each new cloud instance for use as the Puppet certificate's common name. Prepare your base image with a simple `puppet.conf` file that has only the `[main]` section and no `certname` option. Your bootstrapping script then just needs a minor extension:

```
#!/bin/bash
export PATH=/bin:/usr/bin
if ! grep -q ^certname /etc/puppet/puppet.conf ; then
    CERT=`cat /proc/sys/kernel/random/uuid`
    echo "certname = $CERT" >>/etc/puppet/puppet.conf
else
    CERT=`puppet agent --configprint certname`
fi
DIR=`puppet agent --configprint certdir`
[ -f "${DIR}/${CERT}.pem" ] && exit 0
puppet agent --onetime --no-daemonize --waitforcert 300
```

 Such nondescript certificate names make it difficult to recognize possible rogue CSRs. To regain at least some security, you can add the DNS name to the CSR as a **custom attribute**. More on this topic (and actual security) is covered in the *Preparing for autoscaling* section later in this chapter.

With the common names being of no consequence, you might be tempted to take the pragmatic approach of just signing one all-powerful certificate per role and share it among all your cloud agents. This would also appear to avoid all the signing hassle. However, it is not a safe thing to do. Security concerns aside, the assumption that certificate names are unique to each agent runs pretty deep within Puppet. PuppetDB uses `$certname` for one, and we will discuss the importance of this tool for an effective cloud manifest in the next section.

Creating a distributed catalog

If you can manage to design your cloud service in a fashion that allows each instance to fend for itself, consolidated by load balancing, then you can possibly skip this section. On the other hand, the nodes that participate in your cloud service might need to interact in some capacity. You might want to configure a message queue for some or all of your instances. It might be useful if your instances could issue commands to their peers via SSH. You might even want to implement custom load balancing using HAproxy or Nginx if the cloud provider's load balancing is not adequate for any reason.

In all latter scenarios, you need all of your instances to form a mesh of scalable subservices. The whole system must be able to cope with instances leaving and joining at arbitrary times. Ideally, there will not be very tight time constraints for the system to adapt to such changes; you just have to make sure that everything works in an acceptable time frame.

These requirements technically boil down to one necessity: Puppet needs to maintain some parts of each instance's configuration with details about the other nodes. You implemented such structures while working through a previous chapter; Puppet supports this kind of distributed knowledge in the form of exported resources.

You shared some useful commodities such as SSH host keys and entries in host files through exported resources, and you also shared more critical configuration items such as firewall rules or the Nagios configuration snippets. By combining both approaches (the distribution of information over the whole range of agents and the incorporation of specific addresses and metainformation in running software configurations), Puppet's exported resources allow you to implement just the required mesh of interdependent service instances.

The exported firewall rule is a good example for the archetype of an exported resource. It distributes several pieces of information to nodes that concern themselves with them:

- The most important information is almost always the local node's IP address
- The exported resource also carries information on the exporter's capabilities.

In the case of firewall rules, the resource will include one or more ports that the exporter is willing to share. Let's construct a possible resource for your cloud nodes to share among one another. Assume that your cloud employs an SSH-based RPC system that implements simple distributed actions. You configure this system through files in the `/etc/rcmd/<command>.d/` directories, with each file containing one or more IP addresses of SSH servers — one address per line. If required, the remote user can also be specified in the SSH notation as `user@address`. A node that wishes to run a command on all eligible peer nodes can just loop over all addresses from the `<command>.d` directory in question.

Distributing the configuration itself is simple. You can export the files directly, but it is better to wrap them in a defined type that models the semantics:

```
define rcmd::command($runner, $user, $id) {
    file {
        "/etc/rcmd/${name}.d/${id}":
            ensure  => 'file',
            content => "${user}@${runner}\n";
    }
}
```

Now, each node can export its commands in a unified fashion:

```
@@rcmd::command {
    [ 'clear-cache', 'reload-config' ]:
        runner => $ipaddress,
        user   => hiera('rcmd::user', 'rcmd'),
        id     => $clientcert,
}
```

 Note that the facts and Hiera lookups cannot be made into parameter defaults for the defined type. If you did that and the exporting node did not specify these values, then the facts and Hiera data would be looked up by the importing node, which is never the desired outcome.

Each node must manage the available directories for itself. It is useful to use the `file` type's `purge` parameter here so that nodes that no longer appear in the database of exported resources are cleared from the configuration:

```
define rcmd::command_dir() {
    include rcmd::base_dir
    file {
        "/etc/rcmd/${name}.d":
            ensure  => 'directory',
            owner   => 'root',
            mode    => 644,
            recurse => true,
            purge   => true,
    }
}
```

This defined type is used and complemented by the following declarations:

```
rcmd::command_dir { [ 'clear-cache', 'reload-config', … ]: }
# import peer nodes' configs
Rcmd::Command<<| |>>
# also use own exports
Rcmd::Command<| |>
# the class to make sure that /etc/rcmd exists
class rcmd::base_dir {
    file { '/etc/rcmd': ensure => directory, ... }
}
```

This would suffice to build the network of SSH servers, but there is one detail still missing. Each node must be authorized to build an appropriate SSH connection in the first place. The easiest way to make this happen is a preshared key. It is easy to supply the private key to all cloud nodes through Puppet's `file` type:

```
file {
    '/root/.ssh/id_rsa.rcmd':
        owner  => 'root',
        mode   => '600',
        source => 'puppet:///modules/rcmd/root/.ssh/id_rsa.rcmd',
}
```

The public key can be easily authorized for the scripting user through the `ssh_authorized_key` resource:

```
ssh_authorized_key {
    'rcmd-key':
        ensure => 'present',
        type   => 'rsa',
        user   => hiera('rcmd::user'),
        key    => hiera('rcmd::public_key'),
}
```

By updating the master with new public keys in Hiera, you can also easily perform staggered key rotations. The agent will add new authorized keys alongside the old ones, provided that you give them a new resource name. Obsolete keys can be explicitly removed through `ensure => absent` or overwritten with new keys.

Composing arbitrary configuration files

Many services allow configuration through directories that represent some variation on the `conf.d` pattern. All files found in such a directory get concatenated to form the whole configuration. We implemented such a scheme for the SSH-based remote command execution facility in just the previous section. If you get the chance to design a configuration scheme yourself, try and go for this pattern. It makes your life much easier and lends itself to Puppet management especially well.

On the other hand, it is not rare for services to require complex configuration in single files. Virtual host definitions for Nginx or Apache form configuration directories, but each one can contain large chunks of configuration that cannot be subdivided. The `http` section in Nginx's configuration must be contained in a single file. The OpenSSH server uses a monolithic configuration file. HAproxy requires one config file per server process. The list goes on.

With its native tools, this means that Puppet will have to manage such files through a single class or defined type; this makes it very difficult to collect exported resources to form a composite configuration. The typical solution to this problem is the puppetlabs-concat module. It allows you to declare any file to be a patchwork of file sections. Puppet will make sure that it rebuilds the file whenever the set of snippets changes or the content of either snippet is updated.

For example, the puppetlabs-apache module models virtual host definitions by concatenating the expansions of several ERB templates populated with values from module parameters. Let's do something that is a little simpler—construct an HAproxy configuration file through the concat module. It will suffice to limit our sample module to support four configuration sections:

```
global
    # server global settings here
defaults
    # settings for both frontend and backend
frontend <%= @title %>
    mode <%= if @use_http_mode then 'http' else 'tcp' end %>
    default_backend <%= @title %>
backend <%= @title %>
    server ID1 address1:port1 maxconn X
    server ID2 address2:port2 maxconn X
    # … one line per backend server here
```

As you can see, the sketch contains ERB tags already, which will go verbatim to the templates that will comprise the backbone of the defined type:

```
define haproxy::config($ensure = 'present',
                       $globals = [ 'daemon' ],
                       $defaults = [ 'timeout connect 10s' ],
                       $use_http_mode = true) {
    concat {
        "/etc/haproxy/${name}.cfg":
            ensure => $ensure;
    }
    Concat::Fragment { target => "/etc/haproxy/${name}.cfg" }
    concat::fragment {
        "haproxy-${name}-globals":
            order   => '10',
            content => template('haproxy/cfg-global.erb');
        "haproxy-${name}-defaults":
            order   => '20',
            content => template('haproxy/cfg-defaults.erb');
```

```
        "haproxy-${name}-frontend":
            order   => '30',
            content => template('haproxy/cfg-frontend.erb');
        "haproxy-${name}-backend-header":
            order   => '40',
            content => "backend ${name}\n"
    }
}
```

The respective `order` parameter makes sure that Puppet concatenates the snippets in the right order. All individual backend servers should appear underneath the `backend header` line and will use `order 50`:

```
define haproxy::backend_server($instance, $address,
                               $port, $maxconn) {
    $line = "server $name ${address}:$port maxconn $maxconn"
    concat::fragment {
        "haproxy-${instance}-backend-${name}":
            target => "/etc/haproxy/${instance}.cfg",
            order  => '50',
            content => "    $line\n",
    }
}
```

Each cloud instance that takes part in a specified load balancing group exports its line to all HAproxy servers:

```
@@haproxy::backend_server {
    $clientcert:
        instance => 'my-balanced-service',
        address  => $ipaddress,
        port     => '3782',
        maxconn  => '24',
}
```

Collecting applicable fragments is easy too:

```
Haproxy::Backend_server<<| instance == 'my-balanced-service' |>>
```

This code allows a cloud to build flexible HAproxy configurations. The design pattern is applicable to many configuration formats and can be ported to most distributed software solutions.

Handling instance deletions

Exported resources are kept in the PuppetDB persistently. If an agent gets decommissioned, its records will usually stay in the database. Manifests that import these resources will continue to regard them as regular exports. For dynamic cloud configuration, this is undesirable (it is not wanted in most contexts, actually).

PuppetDB can *deactivate* records to account for this. The information will still remain available, but the resources will no longer get imported. You can manually deactivate a node when you delete its cloud instance. Use the `puppet node deactivate` command on the PuppetDB server (as the `root user`):

```
puppet node deactivate 849b97f5-872e-4d31-a668-badf678c5b00
```

If you do not want to or cannot perform this step manually, you can also define a time to live for all node records:

```
# in /etc/puppet/puppetdb.conf
node-ttl = 60m
```

If the export information is not regularly renewed within the specified interval, PuppetDB will automatically deactivate the data. Be careful not to set this too low; if an instance checks in late or misses a Puppet run for any reason, its resources would intermittently be missing from the from the catalogs of the nodes that import them.

To clean up the cloud's configuration, you will also have to make sure that resources that leave management are actually removed from the systems. You have already seen how you can keep `conf.d` style directories clean using the `purge` parameter of the `file` resource that manages the directory. The `concat` type automatically tidies up after vanishing fragments in the same fashion, and there is no special parameter that you need to use.

For other native resources, you can try cleaning out the now unmanaged entities using the `resources` type:

```
resources { "sshkey": purge => true }
```

It only works for resources that the agent can easily locate on the managed system. For example, the purging of authorized SSH keys must be configured through the owning `user` type instead, because the `resources` type cannot enumerate them:

```
user {
    'rcmd':
        ensure         => present,
        uid            => '2082',
        purge_ssh_keys => true,
}
```

Also, keep in mind that purging will only work for native resources and not instances of defined types. To clean these up, you will have to target their wrapped resources for purging. You did this already in the `rcmd` example—the `file` resources with the `purge => true` parameter took care of purging unmanaged `rcmd::command` resources by removing the files that the defined type had created.

Preparing for autoscaling

One advantage of cloud computing over classic data center operations is its ability to minimize the cost for infrastructure. You usually don't need to overprovision your cloud server resources, because you can add instances on short notice. If your workload is fluctuating, predictably or not, you can potentially further minimize the infrastructure through autoscaling features. Let the cloud provider add and remove instances as the load increases and decreases again.

With the techniques you have learned already, you can make Puppet perform any required dynamic reconfiguration of the existing nodes and ensure adequate provisioning of the newly created instances. The latter can only work if Puppet can include new agents without manual intervention, though. The following sections describe the possible strategies that make Puppet work in an autoscaling cloud.

Managing certificates

The crux of the problem is that you need a way for your agents to retrieve signed certificates without an operator who supervises the signing process. This can be easily achieved by setting the `autosign` option to `true` on the master. It instructs Puppet to just sign a certificate for any CSR it receives. This is obviously bad security—any agent that can make a connection to your master will receive a trusted certificate and can keep requesting catalogs.

On the other hand, manual signing is not the only alternative. As a more secure compromise, you can implement an **autosigning script** instead. Configure it in Puppet by setting the `autosign` setting to a file path instead of `true`:

```
autosign = /etc/puppet/autosign
```

The script's function is aptly described by Puppet's online reference documentation:

> *"If a custom policy executable is configured, the CA puppet master will run it every time it receives a CSR. The executable will be passed the subject CN of the request as a command line argument, and the contents of the CSR in PEM format on stdin. It should exit with a status of 0 if the cert should be autosigned and non-zero if the cert should not be autosigned."*

This allows you to implement arbitrary criteria that the master can apply to each incoming certificate request. If you use UUIDs as certificate common names, it will be difficult to make a decision based on the data from the CSR. You should, therefore, add more information to the requests so that the master can verify that they originate from authorized agents.

Puppet is prepared to do this through the same feature that allows you to register trusted facts. You can embed arbitrary information in the certificate-signing request, which is indexed with OIDs. There is even a registered OID for just the authorization string we need, `1.3.6.1.4.1.34380.1.1.4`, with the short name `pp_preshared_key`.

 You can learn more about Puppet's support for SSL CSR attributes at `https://docs.puppetlabs.com/puppet/latest/reference/ssl_attributes_extensions.html`.

Just like the cloud instance role, you can issue the PSK to each instance upon deployment. It needs to be added to the `custom_attributes` hash in the `csr_attributes.yaml` file so that it becomes part of the CSR but not of the signed certificate:

```
custom_attributes:
  pp_preshared_key: aiNDN#naCSaiun39nfASnfqwnfsacn!as93ASnfaX
extension_requests:
  1.3.6.1.4.1.34380.1.2.42: appserver
```

The autosign script can just examine the CSR and verify that the PSK is currently valid. You can even do better and defend against spoofing by hashing the key after salting it with the agent's UUID:

```
custom_attributes:
  pp_preshared_key: __HASHED_PSK__
```

The certificate-requesting script can take care of the math involved:

```
#!/bin/bash
export PATH=/bin:/usr/bin
if ! grep -q ^certname /etc/puppet/puppet.conf ; then
    CERT=`cat /proc/sys/kernel/random/uuid`
    echo "certname = $CERT" >>/etc/puppet/puppet.conf
else
    CERT=`puppet agent --configprint certname`
fi
DIR=`puppet agent --configprint certdir`
[ -f "${DIR}/${CERT}.pem" ] && exit 0
```

```
PSK=`cat /path/to/psk`
HASH=`echo "$CERT$PSK" | sha512sum - | cut -d\  -f1`
sed -i s/__HASHED_PSK__/$HASH/ /etc/puppet/csr_attributes.yaml
puppet agent --onetime --no-daemonize --waitforcert 10
rm /path/to/psk
```

The autosign script extracts the CSR attribute and verifies that the current PSK has been used to compute the hash value:

```
#!/bin/bash
CN=$1
PSK=`cat /path/to/psk`
EXPECT=`echo "$CN$PSK" | sha512sum - | cut -d\  -f1`
HASH=`openssl req -noout -text \
      | grep '1\.3\.6\.1\.4\.1\.34380\.1\.1\.4' \
      | cut -d: -f2 | tr -d ' '`
[[ "$HASH" = "$EXPECT" ]]
```

The result of the final equality test decides whether the certificate will be signed.

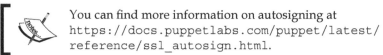

> You can find more information on autosigning at
> https://docs.puppetlabs.com/puppet/latest/
> reference/ssl_autosign.html.

Limiting round trip times

Depending on your configuration, it can take quite a while for newly exported resources to reach all interested agent nodes. The default run interval is half an hour, so this is usually the maximum. In a large cloud, you might even want to increase this interval so that the master is not swamped by frequent catalog requests. This will lead to an increased mean time for distributing configuration details. In a cloud application that uses autoscaling, this might be a painful bargain, because the scaling operations can take a long time to take effect.

You can create a construct that allows Puppet to run in long intervals but react quickly when a change to the network is detected. All you need is a dedicated node with a very simple manifest, which you can afford to compile in a relatively high frequency. This node should import exactly one resource that each of your cloud instances exports, such as their SSH host keys. A change in these resources should trigger a Puppet run across the whole network. The manifest can be constructed as follows:

```
exec { '/usr/local/sbin/trigger-puppet': refreshonly => true }
resources { 'sshkey': purge => true }
```

```
Sshkey<<| |>>         ~> Exec['/usr/local/sbin/trigger-puppet']
Resources['sshkey'] ~> Exec['/usr/local/sbin/trigger-puppet']
```

This is how it works:

1. The exec resource runs the trigger-puppet script only when it receives a signal.

2. SSH host keys are imported from all peers in the cloud, and obsolete keys are purged using the resources type.

3. When a new key gets imported, it sends an event to the exec resource.

4. When one or more keys are purged, a signal is sent to the exec resource.

Now, all you need is the trigger-puppet script that triggers an agent run on all peer nodes. This can be implemented through a custom facility such as the rcmd module that was proposed earlier in this chapter. Another approach is to use a message queue that has been designed for such purposes, such as MCollective, which is yet another tool from the Puppet ecosystem.

Let's create a simple example using rcmd. Every node in your cloud should register itself to receive calls from the Puppet master machine. Make sure that you include this puppet_remote_control::agent class in all manifests:

```
class puppet_remote_control::agent {
    @@rcmd::command {
        'trigger-puppet':
            runner => $ipaddress,
            user   => hiera('rcmd::user', 'rcmd'),
            id     => $clientcert,
    }
}
```

The master node also includes a dedicated class that collects all these call targets:

```
class puppet_remote_control::master {
    Rcmd::Command<<| title == 'trigger-puppet' |>>
    file {
        '/usr/local/sbin/trigger-puppet':
            ensure => 'file',
            mode   => '755',
            source => 'puppet:///modules/puppet_remote_control/
trigger-all-puppet-agents',
    }
}
```

The `trigger-puppet` script is a simple wrapper:

```
#!/bin/sh
/usr/local/sbin/invoke-rcmd trigger-puppet 'sudo puppet agent --test'
```

The `invoke-rcmd` script must be part of the collecting end of the `rcmd` module:

```
class rcmd::invoke {
    file { '/usr/local/sbin/invoke-rcmd': … }
}
```

This class should be included by `define rcmd::command` so that any node that imports a remote command also receives the script. Its content is another simple script:

```
#!/bin/sh
TITLE="$1"
COMMAND="$2"
KEY=/root/.ssh/id_rsa.rcmd
for REMOTE in `cat /etc/rcmd/${TITLE}.d/*` ; do
    ssh -i $KEY $REMOTE "$COMMAND"
done
```

As the command that is called on all remote command runners makes the Puppet agent receive its catalog, you have now created an effective means of updating all your Puppet agents.

Make sure that the Puppet master can cope with the CPU load surge that results from all agents requesting their catalogs. If this is not feasible, you need to complement the agent side of your script with a mechanism that staggers the catalog requests slightly. This allows you to trade the total distribution time for the computing power on the master.

Ensuring successful provisioning

Puppet manifests can fail for a variety of reasons. The compiler can fail to produce a catalog if a syntax error appears. It can also fail if the manifest is inconsistent, with duplicate declarations of the same resource somewhere or other errors. Even if the compilation succeeds, the catalog itself might not apply to all systems cleanly. In this case, you often end up with a partial configuration, because one or more resources fail to sync and all their dependencies are skipped as a result.

This problem is relevant to Puppet agents outside of the cloud as well. However, in your data center, it is usually not a problem to intervene manually in the case of problems. In the cloud, this should be strictly avoided.

Writing Puppet manifests is a form of programming, after all. Producing errors is commonplace. Changes need to be tested properly, and issues require debugging. In the cloud, latent manifest issues are especially annoying, because you might frequently need Puppet to create a complete configuration from scratch. Let's review some rules of thumb that make Puppet as reliable as possible.

 For all the efforts that are described in these final sections, you should still always monitor the agent's operation. Puppet can fail on occasion, but there is no excuse for you not even taking note. If you use PuppetDB, you can just use Puppet Explorer or PuppetBoard to supervise Puppet's work through a web interface.

Adding necessary relationships

Most problems with the application of complete catalogs arise from the wrong ordering of resources. After all, each resource is quite self-contained and can rarely go wrong by itself. However, one resource can often only be synchronized after another. For example, Puppet will enable a service in an idempotent manner by interacting with its start-up script and concerned subsystems. This cannot work if the start-up script cannot be found on the system at the time of resource application. The script is part of the package for the service in question, so the package should be among the service's dependencies.

Keeping resource ordering in mind is key. Always add all dependencies that are necessary. Think carefully about the prerequisites for each resource to be met before it can be queried and possibly brought into sync. This is often easy on a local scale. If your modules can be nicely compartmentalized into relatively small classes, it is often possible to chain all resources in each class into a total order that will always work. The module's main class can take care of ordering the classes, if required.

In a large manifest base, however, there might be more intricate relations. It can happen that a newly developed module works on all machines you use for testing, but only because they have been configured through some other modules already. If the new module is evaluated early during the commissioning of a new instance, it might break because its latent dependencies (upon the older modules) have not been met yet.

The manifest must then be extended to make this dependency explicit (usually by adding the `require` metaparameter to one or more resources) so that Puppet will apply the correct ordering.

Testing the manifests

Such subtle issues are hard to spot in manifests, especially while adding a functionality. You will most likely use a bottom-up strategy to write your manifests and extend new modules step by step until they take the final desired shape. This means that the latter development steps are tested on a machine that is largely configured already so that it is easy to miss possible requirements from inside your own manifest.

To avoid this kind of failure, it is a good idea to stress-test most or all manifest changes. This can be easily done by creating a new temporary virtual machine that uses the manifest in question. If a change affects several roles, you might wish to deploy a test instance for each of these roles.

> In recent versions of Puppet, the ordering of unrelated resources is arbitrary but not random. From a given manifest, the agents will always use the same order of evaluation for the contained resources. So, if your manifest cleanly applies in a test scenario, and you make no further changes, you can be confident that it will keep working flawlessly. You should still be careful about dependency relationships so that manifest changes are not prone to breaking the required orderings.

You will usually not want your test instances to interact with the production instances from your cloud. This can easily happen if you rely on exported resources. It is expected for the test instances to collect resources from production, but exports from the test nodes should generally be ignored by all servers.

You can achieve this through tags. Remember that each resource is tagged with some meta information about the manifest that declares it but can receive additional tags through the `tag` metaparameter. These tags can be arbitrary strings. For example, you can use `production` as a default, unless you have a module or class by that name.

This tag should normally be added to each exported resource, but you need a way to remove it from test instances. A simple way that requires little overhead revolves around the specialized testing of node roles. It also requires you to load the tag from Hiera, where it is defined in the `common` layer:

```
export_tag: production
import_tag: production
```

For each node role, you can add a corresponding test role. The Hiera data source for the respective test role is a carbon copy of production, except that it overrides the `export_tag` value:

```
# role-appserver_test.yaml
export_tag: testing
```

A node using such a role will still export resources, but they will be ignored by all other instances. Make sure that you select the actual tag for all imports:

```
Sshkey<<| tag == hiera('import_tag') |>>
```

The `sshkey` collection is just an example here. The same expression should be used to import all types of resources.

You can even spin up a whole test cloud conceivably if you also override the `import_tag` in the appropriate role data. This would allow you to also test the node interactions, but it should not be necessary under most circumstances.

Summary

The operation of Puppet in the cloud is mostly similar to that in a physical data center. You can cope with the lack of semantic node names by forgoing the classic manifest structure that relies on `node` blocks. The role of each instance can be configured using a Trusted Fact instead. Hiera should ignore hostnames so that roles become the most specific data hierarchy layer.

Certificate signing can be automated and secured through a preshared key. This is convenient for any cloud and an outright requirement if autoscaling is to be supported. Certificates' common names can and should be arbitrary in the cloud. Creating UUIDs for this purpose is a safe choice.

Puppet can keep adapting its catalogs to the cloudscape if you use PuppetDB and enrich your manifests with exported resources. You can collect them into configuration files using the `concat` module. The decommissioning of cloud nodes must then be handled by deactivating their PuppetDB records and purging unmanaged resources from the remaining instances.

To make sure that Puppet successfully configures newly deployed instances, be sure to test your manifests at regular intervals or after important changes. Make sure that all resource dependencies are cleanly specified.

This concludes our tour of *Puppet Essentials*. We have covered quite some ground, but as you can imagine, we only scratched the surface of some of the topics, such as provider development or exploiting PuppetDB. What you have learned will most likely satisfy your immediate requirements. For information beyond these lessons, don't hesitate to look up the excellent online documentation at `https://docs.puppetlabs.com/` or join the community and ask your questions on chat or in the mailing list.

Thanks for reading, and have lots of fun with Puppet and its family of DevOps tools.

Index

O

operatingsystemrelease fact 53
output
  interpreting, of puppet apply
        command 11, 12

P

parameterized classes
  consequences 92, 93
parameters
  versus properties 10
parser functions 96
performance bottlenecks
  avoiding, from templates 136
performance considerations
  about 42
  basic tuning 46
  Passenger, using with Nginx 45
  switching, to Phusion Passenger 43, 44
Phusion Passenger
  switching to 43, 44
  URL, for installation instructions 45
  using, with Nginx 45, 46
Platform as a Service (PaaS) 184
plugins
  about 116
  custom types, creating 118
  custom types, naming 118
  management commands, declaring 121
  provider, adding 121
  provider, allowing to prefetch existing
        resources 123, 124
  provider functionality,
        implementing 122, 123
  resource names, using 120
  resource type interface, creating 119
  sensible parameter hooks, designing 120
  types, making robust 125
  used, for enhancing modules agent 116, 117
plugins, types
  custom facts 116
  parser functions 116
  providers 116
  types 116

processorcount fact 52
properties
  about 10
  versus parameters 10
providerless resource types 61
provider parameter 10
providers
  model, substantiating with 59, 60
  summarizing 61
Puppet
  about 182
  installing 8
  modules 96
  typical scopes 182
  URL 182
Puppet agent
  certificate, renewing 40
  life cycle 38, 39
  running, from cron 41
  setting up 35-37
puppet apply command
  about 9, 31
  output, interpreting of 11, 12
PuppetBoard 186
Puppet Dashboard 186
Puppet Explorer 186
Puppet Labs
  URL 8
  URL, for advanced approaches 43
  URL, for core resource types 61
  URL, for style guide 52
  URL, for system installation information 32
  URL, for Troubleshooting section 47
puppetlabs-strings module
  URL 99
Puppet master
  about 31
  configuration settings, inspecting 35
  master machine, setting up 32
  master manifest, creating 33, 34
  tasks 32
puppetmaster system service 33
puppet module install command 101
Puppet support, for SSL CSR attributes
  URL 199

customization, allowing 113
unwanted configuration items,
   removing 114, 115

V

Vagrant 182
variables
   using 14
variable types
   about 14
   arrays 15
   hashes 14
   strings 15
virtual resources
   creating 137, 138

W

Warning keyword 20

Y

yum command 8

About Packt Publishing

Packt, pronounced 'packed', published its first book "*Mastering phpMyAdmin for Effective MySQL Management*" in April 2004 and subsequently continued to specialize in publishing highly focused books on specific technologies and solutions.

Our books and publications share the experiences of your fellow IT professionals in adapting and customizing today's systems, applications, and frameworks. Our solution based books give you the knowledge and power to customize the software and technologies you're using to get the job done. Packt books are more specific and less general than the IT books you have seen in the past. Our unique business model allows us to bring you more focused information, giving you more of what you need to know, and less of what you don't.

Packt is a modern, yet unique publishing company, which focuses on producing quality, cutting-edge books for communities of developers, administrators, and newbies alike. For more information, please visit our website: www.packtpub.com.

About Packt Open Source

In 2010, Packt launched two new brands, Packt Open Source and Packt Enterprise, in order to continue its focus on specialization. This book is part of the Packt Open Source brand, home to books published on software built around Open Source licenses, and offering information to anybody from advanced developers to budding web designers. The Open Source brand also runs Packt's Open Source Royalty Scheme, by which Packt gives a royalty to each Open Source project about whose software a book is sold.

Writing for Packt

We welcome all inquiries from people who are interested in authoring. Book proposals should be sent to author@packtpub.com. If your book idea is still at an early stage and you would like to discuss it first before writing a formal book proposal, contact us; one of our commissioning editors will get in touch with you.

We're not just looking for published authors; if you have strong technical skills but no writing experience, our experienced editors can help you develop a writing career, or simply get some additional reward for your expertise.

Puppet Reporting and Monitoring

ISBN: 978-1-78398-142-7   Paperback: 186 pages

Create insightful reports for your server infrastructure using Puppet

1. Learn how to prepare and set up Puppet to report on a wealth of data.

2. Develop your own custom plugins and work with report processor systems.

3. Explore compelling ways to utilize and present Puppet data with easy-to-follow examples.

Extending Puppet

ISBN: 978-1-78398-144-1   Paperback: 328 pages

Design, manage, and deploy your Puppet architecture with the help of real-world scenarios

1. Plan, test, and execute your Puppet deployments.

2. Write reusable and maintainable Puppet code.

3. Handle challenges that might arise in upcoming versions of Puppet.

Please check **www.PacktPub.com** for information on our titles

Puppet 3 Cookbook

ISBN: 978-1-78216-976-5   Paperback: 274 pages

Build reliable, scalable, secure, and high-performance systems to fully utilize the power of cloud computing

1. Use Puppet 3 to take control of your servers and desktops, with detailed step-by-step instructions.

2. Covers all the popular tools and frameworks used with Puppet: Dashboard, Foreman, and more.

3. Teaches you how to extend Puppet with custom functions, types, and providers.

Mastering Puppet

ISBN: 978-1-78398-218-9   Paperback: 280 pages

Pull the strings of Puppet to configure enterprise-grade environments for performance optimization

1. Implement Puppet in a medium to large installation.

2. Deal with issues found in larger deployments, such as scaling and improving performance.

3. Step-by-step tutorials to utilize Puppet efficiently to have a fully functioning Puppet infrastructure in an enterprise-level environment.

Please check **www.PacktPub.com** for information on our titles